Kitsch Deluxe

Kitsch Deluxe

LESLEY GILLILAN

MITCHELL BEAZLEY

First published in 2003 by Mitchell Beazley,

an imprint of Octopus Publishing Group Ltd,

2–4 Heron Quays, London E14 4JP

ISBN 1 84000 716 8

A CIP record of this book is available
from the British Library

Commissioning Editor **Emma Clegg**

Executive Art Editor **Auberon Hedgecoe**

Senior Editor **Emily Anderson**

Designers **Emily Wilkinson, Victoria Bevan**

Picture Researchers **Giulia Hetherington, Jenny Faithfull**

Production Controller **Gary Hayes**

Copy Editor **Colette Campbell**

Proofreader **Laura Hicks**

Indexer **Helen Snaith**

Set in NeuzeitS and Daddy-O

Printed and bound in China by

Toppan Printing Company Limited

To order this book as a gift or an incentive contact

Mitchell Beazley on 020 7531 8481

contents

A Brief History of Kitsch

The precise origin of the word "kitsch" is inconclusive, but it is believed to be a derivation of the German slang "etwas verkitschen" meaning "to make cheap" (or "kitschen" – "to collect junk from the street"). It is also thought to date back to the salons of 19th-century Vienna, where it was employed by the art intelligentsia to sneer at the lamentable taste and bourgeois values of the rising middle classes. Thereafter the word slipped into the mainstream of English vocabulary, where it was often used by the middle classes to denigrate the mass-market values of the rising proletariat. In essence, kitsch has almost always been about members of one rank or another assuming superiority by looking down their noses at the excesses and the limitations of popular culture.

Defined in *The Concise Oxford Dictionary* as "worthless pretentiousness in art", kitsch is generally understood to mean cheap and tawdry and is associated with the plastic, the imitation, or, in modern American terminology, the "knock-off". However, for a growing number of people the word is no longer pejorative. There is no dictionary that yet defines kitsch as a cultish modern trend that sees educated aesthetes shamelessly embracing pink-plastic lawn flamingos, plaster poodles, or, indeed, worthless pretentious art, but it has certainly undergone an informal redefinition among an emerging generation of kitsch-lovers, for whom plastic is the new gold.

In this modern context, kitsch encapsulates the ironic "so-bad-it's-good" sensibility, which rejoices in the shortcomings of low-budget B-list movies and low-brow art. As such it also represents a form of inverted snobbery. Kitsch film director John Waters once said, "In order to acquire bad taste, one must first have very, very good taste." Hence, the cognoscenti of kitsch take pains to differentiate between what they see as kitsch and what they see as bad taste. However, for others bad taste doesn't come into the equation: they are simply attracted to playful objets d'art, colourful mass-produced souvenirs, and vivid-themed decor. And then there are those for whom kitsch continues to represent the stereotypes of artificiality and vulgarity. In short, the word is loaded with contradictions and counter-meanings, as complex, and as impossible to define, as taste itself.

I certainly had no inkling of the word when, growing up in the 1950s and '60s, I felt the first stirrings of a populist sensibility, subtly at odds with my immediate environment. I was brought up on Georgian rosewood, Sanderson linens, and 19th-century watercolours, set in a post-war British landscape furnished with good-quality china and decent, middle-class values. Life, nonetheless, was infiltrated with the popular American culture that helped shape the fashions of those distinctive decades. I recall, in particular, the intoxicating Hollywood-movie glamour that seeped from our newly acquired black-and-white TV screen (between episodes of *Tarzan*, *Thunderbirds*, and Lucille Ball's *I Love Lucy* show). I remember the home-interest magazine adverts for easy-wipe dinette kitchens in "jewel-bright" Formica, alongside pictures of boomerang coffee tables, sparkly vinyl cocktail bars, and Sputnik lamps.

I was seduced by the gleaming chrome tail-fins of Ford Zephyrs in candy-floss pink (we had solid sensible Austins and Morrises in staid colours); I read *Bunty* comics under the bedclothes (my parents advocated *Princess* as a more suitable magazine for a young girl); and I was teased for my preference for brushed Bri-nylon sheets (which thankfully I grew out of). In my early teens I finally expressed myself by covering up the flowery walls of my bedroom with a deep shade of purple paint. Did I think it was kitsch? Of course not: in 1969, purple was the colour of high fashion. Indeed, my mother reluctantly endorsed my choice of decor by adding curtains in a mauve-orange-pink abstract number called "Minaret" by Sanderson. My longing for a paisley-print beanbag, or an inflatable chair, was left unrequited.

Much later, I resurrected those curtains – dragged from the brink of extinction, they were swiftly transformed from a musty relic of my growing-up days to a groovy classic of late-1960s pop. They have thus become a fitting accessory of my chosen decor – a fusion of 1950s and 1960s collectables (cocktail glasses, Spanish flamenco dancers, funky lamps, spike-legged furniture), teamed with diner-style kitchenware, bright retro colours, and the odd icon of vintage trash art. The components of this jumbled polyglot of what we now call kitsch are souvenirs of numerous revisits to the decades of my youth. They are products of nostalgia (nostalgia, in particular, for things I remember but did not necessarily have), as well as an expression of those early yearnings for plastic laminates. According to Celeste Olalquiaga, the Chilean author of *The Artificial Kingdom*, "Kitsch is the world as we would like it to be; not as it is ... kitsch is a flight from the present ... an enchanted grotto." Whether that grotto is a relic of nostalgia, a retreat into fantasy, or an Aladdin's cave of cheap knock-offs, is open to individual interpretation. The history of so-called bad taste certainly suggests that kitsch is inspired by generations of escapism.

In 17th- and 18th-century Europe, the merchants of the French and British empires, who rose up the social ladder to become the fat cats

The sets of Pedro Almodovar's 1994 film *Kika* recreated the kitsch decor of the 1950s, complete with George Nelson's classic "Marshmallow" sofa, and leopardskin-print flooring.

A magazine advertisement, dated 1959, for American-style dinette kitchens by English Rose.

French fashions during the reign of Marie Antoinette included extravagantly decorative hairpieces, such as a galleon in full sail.

Parrures des Dames

Cœffure à l'Indépendance ou le Triomphe de la liberté.

of a new aristocracy, tended towards the non-allegorical style of grotto. Alongside Grecian temples, sham castles, and fake ruins, they sprinkled shell-encrusted grottos over their estates in much the same way that later generations decorated their gardens with gnomes. These baroque follies are now lauded as gems of classic landscape architecture, but they are rooted in the same desire for escapism that drives the modern taste for kitsch. Indeed, one fashion among landowners of the day was to build a rustic woodland hermitage and install a ragged, bearded recluse to give flesh to the fantasy.

Pretence of one sort or another is one of the cornerstones of kitsch, and among its early mentors was the last Queen of France, Marie Antoinette (1755–93). Largely responsible for the flamboyant style attributed to her king, Louis XVI, and the ludicrous high-rise hairdos favoured by the ladies of her court, her extravagance earned her the nickname "Madame Deficit". She did not deserve this title entirely, but she certainly had a taste for the whimsical – notably in her Viennese retreat (or "hamean"), where the young Marie Antoinette played at being a simple milkmaid, shepherding flocks of delicately perfumed sheep and goats, and eating from porcelain bowls cast in the shape of her own breasts.

Later, in Germany, Ludwig II, the so-called "mad King" of Bavaria (1845–86), expressed his taste for baroque extravagance by building a series of sumptuous castles, including the famous Schloss Neuschwanstein (which, perhaps, was later to inspire the magical castles of Disneyland). For the shy, nocturnal Ludwig, who was known to travel at night in elaborate sleighs dressed in medieval costume, the mock-medieval Neuschwanstein was a refuge from reality. He was dedicated to the operas of Wagner and the poetic world of the Middle Ages, and the castle was an early exponent of themed decor – a melange of Byzantine, Romanesque, and Gothic styles, with accents of Venus Grotto. Designed to look like a natural dripstone cave, complete with waterfall and coloured lighting, Ludwig's Neuschwanstein grotto was entirely fake.

The century that followed the Industrial Revolution saw huge innovations in mass-production, and the first inkling of a true consumer society. It is not surprising, then, that the Victorians were one of the most taste-obsessed generations in history – a fact that was graphically illustrated in London at the Great Exhibition of 1851. The exhibition, at which a vast array of goods was presented in the Crystal Palace to the people of the British Empire, was the brainchild of Prince Albert and Sir Henry Cole (who later founded the Victoria and Albert Museum). The aim was to show British design and ingenuity at its best, alongside a collection of products from all over the world. It was also a well-meaning attempt to impose the ideals of good taste on the expanding middle classes who, it was feared, were sinking into a morass of excess. However, it didn't quite work out like that.

With 100,000 exhibits, spread over 18 acres under a million square feet of glass, the Crystal Palace exhibition was a gigantic bazaar, as commercial as a modern-day shopping mall (except that the fake foliage was made of cast iron). Even by Victorian standards many of the exhibits were grotesquely over-decorative, but the Great Exhibition was to wield huge influence on Victorian interior design. The typical well-to-do living room (as dictated by Cassell's *Household Guide*, first published 1869) featured an abundance of flowery wallpapers and foliage-sprigged carpets, heavy drapes trimmed with tassels, an example of home taxidermy (a case of take a bird, dismember, stuff, and mount), a parlour aquarium, and the whole skin and teeth of a late, and in those days unlamented, tiger sprawled out in front of a Gothic Revival fireplace. Strangely, Victorian decor is still perceived by many as the mother of traditional British taste.

The 20th century was certainly the mother of kitsch. In a small way it began in the 1930s, with another significant shift in social demography and the rapid rise of the Hollywood phenomenon – the first true manifestation of international celebrity. The films themselves fed dreams and aspirations, but just as significant was Hollywood's ability to transform ordinary people into iconographic superstars. The infamous excesses of movie stardom (the villas, the swimming pools, the gold-dolphin taps) were all part of the alluring, make-believe, Disney-world of Tinseltown.

Despite recession on both sides of the Atlantic, the 1930s also saw one of the largest urban expansions in history. For example,

Pop artist Andy Warhol explored the cult of celebrity in his much-reproduced silk-screened portrait of *24 Marilyns* (1964), and in portraits of other icons of the period.

Back to the Future: Joe Colombo's space-age "central living block", made for the 1969 *Visiona 1* exhibition in Cologne, Germany.

in London the suburban building boom, which increased the housing stock by 30 per cent in less than two decades, gobbled up the city's rural perimeters at an alarming rate. This was the age of Art Deco, and the dawning of machine-age Modernism, but part of the culture of suburbia was to pine for lost rural idylls. Hence, the countrified mock-Tudor architecture, whimsical street names, and one of the most familiar idioms of kitsch – sets of flying ducks.

Flying ducks are also associated with the 1950s, but the New Look decade that followed the Second World War produced much richer seams of pedigree kitsch. This was the age of the drive-in, the diner, the do-it-yourself craze, the jukebox, the jive, cocktail lounges, Californian Tiki bars, and colourful factory-made goods bought on "the never-never" (or easy-pay credit terms). For the first time, ordinary working-class people had money to spend on cars, holidays, homes, and furniture, and, after the drudgery and austerity of the war years, they wanted fun, excitement, and, above all, colour. This pent-up demand exploded in a feast of consumer goods in abstract shapes, bright patterns, and fantastic new materials such as plastic laminates and vinyl.

In London the apotheosis of the new design decade was the Festival of Britain in 1951 – a celebration of "gaiety, colour and enchantment" spread out over 27 acres of bombed-out wasteland on the south bank of the River Thames. With contributions from some of the most talented young designers, artists, and architects of the time, the festival featured a Dome of Discovery, a rocket-like "Skylon", dozens of themed pavilions, and kitsch-fantasy pleasure gardens. The Festival of Britain style – all twiddles of wrought iron, spikes, molecules, structural geometry, and fondant colours – made a huge impact on British design in the 1950s. Yet the true spirit of the decade belonged essentially to the USA.

Alongside classic examples of 1950s design, such as George Nelson's Ball Clock (inspired by atomic science), and his "Marshmallow" sofa, the post-war American dream produced a sea of tacky plastic fakery, from leopardskin print and vinyl leatherette to a mélange of Polynesian and Hawaiian styles, as well as some of the most inspirational pop icons of the century – Elvis, Marilyn Monroe, and Jayne Mansfield among them. On both sides of the Atlantic the 1950s was the kitsch aesthetic's pivotal moment – a rich concentration of whimsy, the like of which has never been seen before or since.

In the "Space Age" 1960s (also known as the "Swinging Sixties"), the consumer society became more sophisticated, more technologically advanced, and significantly younger, from the Op Art mod in kinky boots and mini skirt to the hippy-dippy flower child. One of the most democratic design periods of the last century, its Pop Art movement broke down traditional boundaries between high- and low-brow culture, and blurred the distinctions between fine art and commercial design. Artists, and in particular Andy Warhol, took their inspiration from advertising, comics, cartoons, science-fiction, and the cult of celebrity. In interior design, the 1960s was a decade that saw itself as progressive but loved to escape into the future (hence the kitsch collectables of the period tend towards *Barbarella*-style futuristic pop, such as lava lamps and space-ball televisions). Danish designer Verner Panton's space-agey, neo-modern furniture in vivid freeform plastics sums up the spirit of the age.

The flamboyance of Italian design was also a massive influence, producing among other things the inflatable Blow chair, and the Sacco chair (a vinyl sleeve filled with polystyrene pellets – the mother of the beanbag). Meanwhile the notions of modern good taste were undermined by emerging anti-design groups. Archizoom Associati, formed in 1966 by architect Andrea Branzi, expressed this trend in a series of fantasy furnishings, such as the "Dream Bed" – a fusion of surrealism, Art Deco, fake leopardskin, and pop motifs.

For some, the 1970s is the ultimate decade of kitsch. It began with a hangover of the psychedelic movement (lurid abstractions of drug-induced colour), and woke up to glam rock and glittery hot-pants, before going down with a bad case of disco fever (cured by a dose of anarchic punk rock). Towards the end of the decade it also saw the first flowering of kitsch – the tongue-in-cheek kind of kitsch that takes a subversive delight in enjoying aspects of life that were previously upheld as the epitome of poor taste. It was too early to lampoon the excesses of the decade in which it was born (the orange bathroom suites, the shag-pile carpet, the big hair), but it became amusing and clever to send

The 1967 prototype Dream Bed, by Italian anti-design group Archizoom, drew inspiration from Hollywood glamour, kitsch, and popular culture.

☞ This 1970s bathroom encapsulates the taste for shag-pile carpet and vivid colour during the "Disco Decade".

up the 1950s, to collect flying ducks, or watch re-runs of *I Love Lucy* shows. Original 1960s *Star Trek* episodes, I recall, became a huge favourite, not for the gripping plots and special effects, but for the wooden acting and unrealistic quasi-futuristic sets.

This frivolous new mood was, in part, a product of Post-modernism – a reaction to the austerity of functional, rational modernism, which was described by Viennese architect Friedrich Hundertwasser as "like painting with a ruler". Post-modernism took a witty, unrestrained, anything-goes approach to design, which was anti-technology, anti-mass-production, and pro-decoration. At the forefront of the movement was the design group Studio Alchimia. Founded in 1976 by Milan-based Austrian designer Ettore Sottsass, and Alessandro Mendini, the editor of *Modo* and *Domus* magazines, the group discarded preconceived ideas of good or bad taste by experimenting with the kitsch and the banal, mixing new and traditional materials, and vivid combinations of primary colour.

In 1981 Ettore Sottsass went on to found the Memphis Group – a band
of like-minded designers (Matteo Thun, Marco Zanini, and Michele de
Lucchi), who extended the principles of Post-modernism with experimental
products and furniture, which had a playful, toylike quality. Typical is the
iconographic "Casablanca" sideboard, designed by Sottsass for the
1981 Milan Fair – a bizarre creature clad in plastic laminate,
printed with Sottsass' 1950s-style "Bacterio" pattern.

The work of French super-designer Philippe Starck carried
the spirit of Post-modernism into the 1990s, with added science-
and-technology, dramatic use of light, and organic forms. Starck has
dabbled in the whimsical too, notably in a *fin de siècle* generation of
European hotel foyers. For example, the foyer of London's St Martin's
Lane Hotel opened in 1998 with a surreal mix of giant vases, over-sized
gilt chairs, and stools shaped like gold teeth and garden gnomes.
However, in general, the 1990s was a decade of design snobbery and
control-freak minimalism, and high-maintenance, monochrome interiors
religiously furnished with glass, steel, and black leather, occasionally
lifted with a splash of taupe.

By the end of the century an antidote to designer minimalism
emerged in a "less is a bore" school of home furnishing – a rash of
1950s-style shocking pinks, acid greens, and electric blues, a renaissance
of 1960s-style fun furniture, and a new taste for frivolous kitsch. More
affectionate than ironic, the latter is fuelled by a growing interest in
mass-produced 20th-century collectables, as well as by the rise of the
"tweeny" (or young-teenage) consumer. This trend has seen the re-issue
of works of art formerly known as trash, a new generation of blow-up
chairs, nodding dogs, and lava lamps, and a niche market in kitsch
retailing. Followers of fashion can refer to a loose vocabulary of icons
and idioms that are, perhaps, essential to the look, but the allure of
the modern kitsch aesthetic is in the lack of rules.

The self-expressive 21st-century "über kitsch" embraces all
forms of escapism, from mock-baroque fantasies and fake takes on
the 1950s, to themed dream decor and bizarre experiments with bright
paintwork and recycled junk. Not to everyone's taste perhaps, but the
ultimate in Kitsch Deluxe.

The post-modern
"Casablanca" sideboard,
designed by Ettore
Sottsass for the
Memphis show in Milan
in 1981, is clad in 1950s-
style plastic laminate.

Icons
of
Kitsch

classic cocktails (Manhattan, Martini, Gin Fizz) date from the late 19th century, but much of the rigmarole associated with cocktail-making is a product of the 20th century, particularly of the 1950s – the age of Pina Coladas, Mai Tais, and Margaritas, mixed at home at spangled, padded vinyl bars, furnished with pineapple ice buckets, novelty glasses, and umbrella cocktail sticks.

Indeed, the 1950s fashion for at-home cocktail parties is responsible for more items of fun bad taste than almost anything else in the kitsch vocabulary. A variety of popular exotic themes (Spanish or Hawaiian, for example), inspired whimsical, now collectable, ranges of cocktail shakers, swizzle sticks, bottles, coasters, and corkscrews, as well as bars and bar stools. A favourite British model was the ship-shaped bar by English company Barget; decked in wood-look laminate and vinyl, it featured portholes, a light-up cabin for displaying glasses, and a below-deck hold for bottles of ready-mixed drinks like Babycham, Snowball, and Cherry B. Martini, anyone?

J.H. Lynch

Popular artist of the 1970s; best known for framed reproductions of his "dusky maiden" paintings including: Gypsy Girl, Autumn Leaves, Woodland Goddess, Tanya, Tara, *and* Tina. Although little is known about the painter John H. Lynch, his Gauguin-meets-girlie-comic school of art was brought to a mass-market audience through the volume sale of chainstore prints. The Lynch oeuvre (voluptuous babes hanging around in woodlands wearing little

☞ Listing to starboard, and laden with treasures, this ship-shaped cocktail bar is a 1950s classic by Barget. The framed print to the stern is *Tina*, the famous "dusky lady" by low-brow artist J.H. Lynch.

☝ Fake flowers (such as these plastic light-up tulips) and jungle prints are among the essential idioms of the kitsch aesthetic.

Cocktails

Art and ritual of mixing and consuming inebriating concoctions of spirits and sweet tropical juices (shaken or stirred); umbrellas optional.

The term "cock tail" was first seen in print in New York in 1806 when the editor of *Balance and Columbian Repository* defined it as a "stimulating liquor, composed of drinks of any kind, sugar, water and bitters". Many of the

more than mascara, lip gloss, and hairspray) was more pin-up than portraiture, but his work found its way into millions of living rooms in the late 1960s and early 1970s. Probably his best-known work is *Tina*, a naked tree-hugger, known to cognoscenti of kitsch as "the dusky maiden" or "the blue lady" (as in soft-porn pose against blue-hued early evening sky).

Cowboys and Cowgirls

Call of the American Wild West; expressed in cowboy-themed memorabilia of the B-movie era. Hollywood's prolific output of cowboy movies and old-fashioned TV Westerns left a long trail of Wild West clichés, instantly recognizable to anyone born before 1970. Thereafter, a new breed of hero – more exciting than the Lone Ranger, younger than John Wayne – made cowboy legends a thing of the past, thereby fuelling a trade in nostalgia. Interest in cowboy memorabilia (gun holsters, chaps, hats, fringed leather, movie posters, cowboy-boot lamps, etc), is often a girl thing (girls, perhaps, who long to play the sharp-shooting heroine of *Annie Get Your Gun*). Cowboys were a popular theme of bedroom textiles for boys in the 1950s–'60s, but girls, too, tend to go for "Cowboy" – a popular retro-style print by contemporary British textile designer Cath Kidston.

Diners

Retro icon of American roadside life; all coloured Formica, chrome, and neon; served with eggs (sunny-side up), Jerry Lee Lewis, and homefries. There is nothing intrinsically kitsch about the

The cowgirl's in the pink as she lights up the Las Vegas sky with a colourful glow of night-time neon.

The classic American diner feeds the fashion for dinette booths, leatherette upholstery, chrome, and coloured Formica.

classic diner, but characteristic features of this quintessentially American icon feed the kitsch aesthetic – by inspiring 1950s-style kitchens, furnished with chrome and stainless steel, coloured vinyl, and Formica, with Art Deco accents.

The first roadside diner, or "luncher", was a horse-drawn vehicle attributed to Rhode Island in 1872. The more familiar diner concept developed in the 1930s, and proliferated in the 1950s. In its purest form, it consists of a factory-made modular structure, built like a car, with a steel body and a ready-to-roll interior, complete with counter, stools, booths, and dinette tables. All you had to do was add the jukebox and the espresso machine.

Most of the leading names in early diner manufacture (Silk City, Mountain View, Sterling, Swingle) are history, but a few survive: Paramount (born 1937) and Diner Mite (1959) are still in production; and in 1989, old-hand Kullman Industries (1927) launched a chain of retro-style, modular "Silver Diners". Branching into Europe, one new Kullman classic has reached Germany.

Neon

Atmospheric gas discovered in 1898; neon ("new gas", from Greek "neos") used as generic term for "positive column discharge lamps". Common medium for street signage; also known as "liquid fire".
In essence, neon lighting is a slender tube of transparent material (usually glass) filled with

neon (an inert atmospheric gas) that glows when energized by an electric charge. Neon itself glows a luminous red, but a complete spectrum of colours can be made by applying voltage to combinations of neon, argon, mercury, and phosphor; the transparent tubes, meanwhile, can be fashioned into any shape, thereby providing endless scope for glowing polychrome artistry in the field of flashy, fluorescent signage.

The first neon lamp was exhibited in Paris in 1910 by French chemist Georges Claude, who was the first to demonstrate its illuminative qualities. Under the name Claude Neon he later introduced neon gas lighting to the United States by selling two signs to a car dealership in Los Angeles in 1923. The rest, as they say, is history. And what an illustrious history: where would Las Vegas be without neon light? However, neon is no longer the leading light of nocturnal street-life. Usurped by computerized LEDs (Light Emitting Diodes), surviving neons are becoming retro classics, destined to be collectors' items and museum pieces.

Religious Kitsch

Souvenirs of the religious experience in glowing visions of gilded plastic; also known as "God kitsch".
O Lord, forgive us for engraving thine image on cheap 3D wall clocks, or dress-me-up fridge magnets; but remember that the market for glow-in-the-dark Madonnas, Jesus memo boards, and other unholy trinkets of a deliberately sacrilegious nature, is inspired by the gift-shop merchandise of the genuinely devout. Follow the well-worn trail of the faithful – a pilgrimage

to Lourdes, perhaps, or a homage to Papal Rome – and the path is lined with statuettes of the Virgin with light-up halos. Kitsch they may be, but Last Supper clocks, stone-finish guardian-angel candles, and Sacred Heart Jesus prints are all available from a gift shop in Vatican City.

☞ To collectors of religious kitsch anything goes, from Sunday-school Madonna figurines and vintage religious imagery, to cheap, gift-shop souvenirs.

Royals

Royal souvenirs, depicting Her Majesty Queen Elizabeth II and family, camped up in State regalia, crowns, and ermine (plus corgis).

British Royal Family memorabilia, largely produced to commemorate pivotal moments in history, tends to appeal to the flag-waving patriot; but there is something here to fit the kitsch aesthete, too. As a rule of thumb, forget the commemorative Golden Jubilee mugs (2002), and the miniature state coaches, and go for vintage relics of the Coronation (1953), or the Silver Jubilee (1977), as well as soft-focus chainstore portraits of Her Majesty clad in post-war Norman Hartnell and Crown Jewels.

Anarchists or republicans might go for the Sex Pistols' *God Save the Queen* posters (complete with safety-pin nose-piercing) by Vivienne Westwood and Jamie Reid. Hopeless romantics might hanker for souvenirs of the doomed union between Charles and Diana (also known as "Chasdi" memorabilia, it includes tea caddies and biscuit tins featuring 1981 pre-nuptial portraits). Obsessives could end up like Margaret Tyler, whose collection of royal memorabilia has turned her suburban London home into a small museum crammed with royal souvenirs, a full-size cardboard cut-out of the Queen (in headscarf), and corgis everywhere.

Wireware

Fancy metalwork of the 1950s; associated with post-war Festival of Britain style (aka wireware with knobs on).

Chrome-plated and plastic-coated wire, steel, or brass rods, and fine wrought iron were the raw materials of a 1950s fashion for spindly metallic homewares (spike-legged chairs, whimsical wall sculptures, and skeletal wire figures).

The style was cheapened by copy-cat mass-production, but its background was in classic mid-century modern design: The Ball Clock by George Nelson (1947), Harry Bertoia's wire-mesh Diamond Chair (1952), and the steel-framed, ball-footed Antelope Chair designed by Ernest Race for the Festival of Britain (1951) were major influences behind the post-war fashion for wireware. The look was further popularized by the 1950s "Atomic Age" style, based on molecular structures, and comprised of wands, wires, and blobs of coloured plastic, or "cocktail cherry" feet (as seen in zigzag wall tidies, hall stands, and magazine and record racks of the period).

Post-war classics: Festival of Britain-style zigzag wireware (with knobs on), and a 1953 Coronation portrait of Her Majesty.

THE CHINESE GIRL
BY TRETCHIKOFF

Tretchikoff

Vladimir Griegorovich Tretchikoff, born in Siberia, 1913. Doyen of low-brow, chainstore art, mass-produced as affordable prints. Best known for Chinese Girl, *1952 (aka "The Green Lady").*

The work of artist Vladimir Tretchikoff, famed for his stylized portraits of exotic women, has never been accepted by the serious art world as anything other than worthless trash.

British art critic William Feaver once referred to Tretchikoff's *Chinese Girl* (known as "The Green Lady" because of her so-tinted complexion) as "the most unpleasant work to be published in the 20th century". He scoffed at her flat hair and the artist's "muzzy line-work", but Tretchikoff's public thought differently.

During the 1950s and '60s, millions of his prints were sold all over the world. The *Chinese Girl* was not only the most reproduced work of the 20th century, but she and her multicoloured sisters (*Balinese Girl, Miss Wong,* etc) also made Tretchikoff the richest artist after Picasso.

In the 1980s Tretchikoff's girls began to make the transition from over the mantelpiece to the dustbin, but they were soon resurrected. "The Green Lady", now the goddess of kitsch, has appeared on the sleeve of an album of elevator music, spawned Green Lady drag artists, and inspired mouse mats, table mats, coffee-table coasters, and light-switch covers. A new generation of "Tretch" prints is selling well, and the price of 1950s originals has soared. Collectors prefer early prints in cheap period frames with a Boots or Woolworths label.

Gnomes

Dwarfish spirit of subterranean race (or "guardian of the earth's treasures"); product of Scandinavian mythology, transmogrified as garden ornament in the form of small bearded men performing menial outdoor tasks.

These dwarf-like figures first appeared in Germany in the form of porcelain *gnomen-figuren* designed as shelf ornaments. They were introduced to Britain, circa 1850, by Sir Charles Isham, who created a personal gnomery in an Alpine rockery in the garden of his home, Lamport Hall in Northamptonshire. Sir Charles' gnomes were not made for outdoor life, but a more robust version soon appeared on the market.

Vladimir Tretchikoff's sultry *Chinese Girl* was painted in 1952. The *Mona Lisa* of low-brow art, prints were reproduced by the million in the decade that followed.

A grinning gnome with fellow garden ornament, the flamingo – seen here as a string of outdoor fairy lights.

Sci-fi heroine, *Barbarella* (Jane Fonda) camps it up in a 41st-century spaceship, lined with 1960s shag pile.

Barbarella

Heroine of 1968 sci-fi movie, based on adult comic strip by Jean-Claude Forest; directed by Roger Vadim and starring his then wife, Jane Fonda, as Barbarella, Queen of the Galaxy.

It was a film that Jane Fonda would have preferred to forget, but her starring role as a wide-eyed, intergalactic space kitten with Barbie hairdo inspired a cult following that proved hard to shake off. And, as a classic of the so-bad-it's-good category of sci-fi movies, *Barbarella* still evokes the fashions and free-love mood of the Swinging Sixties – albeit in a camped-up, outer-space kind of way.

The *Barbarella* story follows the adventures of a "five-star, double-rated, astronautical aviatrix", sent from Earth on a 41st-century mission to find renegade scientist Duran Duran, inventor of the deadly positronic ray (and, later, the inspiration for the 1980s pop band of the same name).

In an Alpha 7 spaceship, lined with orange shag pile, she crash-lands three times, does a zero-gravity striptease, and has casual sex with a blind angel (complete with wings), before encountering a cast of bizarre characters in the plastic city of Sogo. Like a cosmic Alice in Wonderland, she wanders into a psychedelic Chamber of Dreams, is attacked by carnivorous dolls, and escapes the deadly ecstasy of an Excessive Machine. Oh yes, and who could forget the clothes? Costume designer Jacques Fonteray helped "put the gal into galaxy" with a wardrobe of sexy outfits including a diaphanous astro-suit (with hot-pants), feather boa, black lamé, shiny plastic knee-high boots, and shredded fish-nets.

In 1908 the Wahliss Galleries in London's Oxford Street were advertising "gnomes and quaint mannekins ... which lend themselves particularly well for the artistic decoration of parks and gardens". The gnomes on offer were imported from Germany, and were largely made of expensive, hand-painted white terracotta.

When the sole survivor of Sir Charles' collection made a guest appearance at the Chelsea Flower Show in 1993, he was insured for £1 million. But the chap has little in common with the garish, Disney-eyed gnomes of modern suburbia; nor, indeed, with the products of a modern reinterpretation of gnomery in the form of playfully ironic fairy lights, candles, and, notably, furniture by French super-designer Philippe Starck. The Starck gnomes, Attila, Napoleon, and Saint Esprit, were produced in 1999 for the foyer of the St Martin's Lane Hotel in London. Used as stools or occasional tables, they were designed for indoor or outdoor use.

Shag Pile

Loosely constructed carpeting with long-cut surface yarns; metaphor for 1970s style (synonymous with Farrah Fawcett haircuts and Afghan hounds).

Although shag-pile carpet was around at least two decades earlier (Jayne Mansfield covered areas of her late-1950s Hollywood house in pink shag pile), it is more readily associated with the excesses of the 1970s, when it was often seen in various shades of brown and orange (invariably at the same time). In its day, wall-to-wall shag pile (also known as "luxury long pile") denoted a certain air of decadence (white or black shag pile used extensively in a bedroom, for example, suggested an Austin Powers lifestyle); but a floor-covering that needed regular grooming was never going to stay in fashion for long. Shag pile is still around, but normally confined to the sparing use of shaggy wool rugs in modern colours.

Thunderbirds

Supermarionated sci-fi puppet show (1964–66), created by British television producer Gerry Anderson (also responsible for Captain Scarlet, Joe 90, Stingray, *and* Fireball XL5*).*

"The year is 2065. On an island somewhere in the Southern Pacific lies the headquarters of the top secret organization International Rescue. Their mission? To save the world from disaster ..." Or to put it another way: The year is 1963. In a film studio somewhere in Slough, film-producer Gerry Anderson dreams up a cast of string-puppet superheroes, with Bondaglass bodies, electronic vocals, and nylon hair. His mission? To create a 32-episode, supermarionated adventure series,

based around a global rescue service run by Sean Connery-lookalike Jeff Tracy, his five sons (all named after real-life American astronauts), and a big-eyed boffin called Brains. The most successful of Anderson's retro-futuristic animations, *Thunderbirds* still commands an international cult following, particularly among adult fans with fond memories of low-tech puppetry, hammy scripts, and wobbly rockets launched from the polystyrene cliffs of Tracy Island. Characters like the unforgettable Lady Penelope Creighton-Ward (based on Anderson's wife Sylvia) – a secret agent with a pink Rolls Royce, registration FAB 1, chauffeured by Parker ("you rang, milady?") – have ensured that *Thunderbirds* are still Go.

The *Thunderbirds* superheroes (Brains, Virgil Tracy, and brother, Gordon) on another supermarionated rescue mission, circa 2065.

Madonna Inn

Legendary Californian motel, featuring 109 "very special guest rooms", on Highway 101 at San Luis Obispo. Founded by Phyllis and Alex Madonna, 1958. The queen of the themed hotels, the Madonna Inn is an ersatz collection of look-at-me roadside buildings of a style that defies description (try Flintstones-meets-Tyrolean-chalet with mock-Tudor accents). It was built by Alex Madonna, a road construction millionaire (hence the "pick and shovel" trademark), for his wife Phyllis in 1958. The Madonnas took responsibility for the interiors after arguing with decorators, and came up with a sugary pink concoction of boulders, Bavarian carving, cupids, red leather, gold filigree, flock wallpaper, and twinkling lights.

Some of the most striking features reflect Mr Madonna's affinity with large chunks of masonry, as seen in the gents' rockery restrooms, where a waterfall gushes over a man-made cliff-face. "Millions of tourists … [have] made the trip to check out the men's urinal," writes Phyllis in her Madonna Inn biography *My Point of View* (Pick and Shovel, 2002).

However, the Inn is most famous for its 109 themed bedrooms, many of which remain unchanged since Phyllis kitsched them up in the 1960s. Guests can choose from Edelweiss (a tribute to *The Sound of Music*), Krazy Dazy (shocking pink and daisies), Love Nest (screaming pink and chintz), Safari (Witco and wild animals), or 14 cave-like rock rooms including Jungle Rock, Rock Bottom, and The Caveman – so popular with honeymooners that it gets booked up years in advance.

Tropical Fish

Exotic species of lagoon life; housed in simulated oceanic scenery (aka domestic aquarium); also popular motif of decorative homewares. The tropical-fish tank, casting a glow of eerie blue light against a corner of dubious dining-room wallpaper, used to be a cliché of down-market bed-and-breakfast establishments in England. The fish, of course, were always gorgeous (a mesmeric spectacle of iridescent blues and yellows, shimmying through luminous waters), but the tanks themselves were (or are) often furnished with gloriously tacky plastic trinkets (divers, deep-sea treasure, ship-wrecks, etc). It's a style of aquarium decor that

For a wild night at the Madonna Inn in San Luis Obispo, California, "The Caveman" room offers primitive rock walls and jungle prints.

The lounge at Butlins in Bognor Regis (complete with underwater view of an indoor swimming pool), as depicted in a photographic postcard produced by the John Hinde Studio.

started in Victorian times (when sub-aquatic life was as mysterious and as alien as outer space), though earlier forms of bucolic subterranean fantasies (ruined castles, grottos, relics of lost civilizations) were just as tasteless.

Notwithstanding the fact that there is something intrinsically tasteless about keeping tropical fish in an artificial environment, fish tanks have gone up a notch in the world, and are often seen in the lobbies of hip hotels (either real, or as simulated computer images), or as fish-filled glass features in expensive penthouse apartments. However, lapses of taste survive, such as the "Aquariass" aquarium toilet by Oliver Beckert, in which a see-through

acrylic cistern doubles as a live-fish tank (the perfect partner for all those fishy kitsch bathroom accessories).

Butlins

Chain of working-class British holiday camps, founded by Billy (aka Sir William) Butlin in 1936; inspiration for the fictional "Maplins" in the BBC comedy series Hi-De-Hi *(1980–88).*

A cross between a retro Disneyland and an army barracks, Butlins Holiday Camps provided cheap, all-weather family holidays in a choice of nine UK seaside resorts including Skegness, Clacton, Bognor Regis, Minehead, Filey, and Barry. An escape from the grey seas and overcast

during its 1960s heyday slept in prefabricated chalets arranged in military rows around municipal-style playgrounds. Supervised by "Redcoat" staff, they passed the time in vast entertainment hangars (where grown-ups danced the night away on Marley-tiled ballroom floors under corrugated iron roofs); and when summoned by loudspeaker announcements, they filed into noisy dining rooms to eat pie and chips under trellises of plastic flowers. The concept had had its day by the time Billy Butlin sold his empire in 1972, but despite further decline (only three of the original Butlins survive) there remains a deep affection for this British institution. A thriving trade in memorabilia reflects a wistful nostalgia for the seas of primary-coloured Formica and oceans of swirly carpet that encapsulate the Knickerbocker-Glory days of the post-war British holiday.

Dogs ...

Carnivorous quadruped of genus canis; *pet subject of kitsch ornamental art and novelties.* The four-legged doggie friends who have made it into the lexicon of kitsch include corgis (*see* Royals), various breeds of nodding dog (an enduring 1950s classic, originally made in nylon-furred plastic for parcel shelves on the back seats of cars), and Lassie (star of collie-centric 1943 movie *Lassie Come Home*, and lookalikes reproduced on chocolate boxes).

If you prefer chi-chi Parisian-style, just add a poodle. Indeed, the ubiquity of vintage poodle paraphernalia makes this groomed breed of pooch the Crufts champion of canine kitsch.

☞ Cute fluffy pussycats portrayed on a printed-tin litter bin, and a plastic kitty money box.

skies of an unreliable British summer, they offered brightly coloured Beachcomber bars with fake tropical landscapes, mock-Tudor pubs, coffee lounges, tepid indoor pools, miniature railways, fun fairs, games, and talent competitions. The enduring images of girls in bikinis and white stilettos lining up for poolside beauty contests convey a vague glamour – but the reality was rather less alluring. The millions of "campers" who signed up for a Butlins holiday

Look out for pom-pommed poodle bookends, lamp bases, handbags, glassware, and the classic miniature white (or black) mantelpiece poodle with sparkling diamanté eyes.

... and Cats

Small furry domesticated carnivorous quadruped (felis catus); inspiration for cute kitty-kat kitsch.

As with dogs, cat-inspired kitsch saw its heyday in the 1950s and '60s – notably in a Siamesey breed of feline china ornaments with elongated necks and big oval eyes. Similarly-styled black velour cats were part of the packaging for some perfumes such as "Primitif" and "Hypnotique" by Max Factor. Cats were also a popular theme of rhinestone and diamanté brooches, as were soft-focus fluffy kittens, portrayed as cute calendar pin-ups. Among cat-kitsch of the modern age is the ubiquitous Hello Kitty (a product by Sanrio, Japanese specialists in "character-branded stationery"), and fashion phenomenon French Kitty, a retro-style cartoon glamour-puss, or "sophisticat", which looks uncommonly like those long-necked cats of the last century.

Fake Flowers

Nature's ephemeral beauties (roses, tulips, etc) immortalized in durable plastic or printed silk.

Flowers and foliage that grow dusty but never die are one of the essential idioms of kitsch decoration. In the 1950s plastic floristry (which furnished almost anything, from toilet-roll holders to the interiors of diaphanous plastic pouffes) was the last word in bad taste. A certain sense of irony, therefore, is integral to the modern ubiquity of, say, light-up tulips, frivolous flower-sprigged handbags, or curtains of trailing silk blooms. The key to a true kitsch aesthetic is to avoid overt realism. With flowers it has to be proud-to-be-plastic fakery or the real thing.

Flying Ducks

Duck-shaped ceramic wall plaques usually available in threes; reminiscent of wild Mallard drake (anas platyrhyncos); metaphor for English suburban decor of the 1930s and beyond.

Sets of three flying ducks (in small, medium,

Cocktail-bar shelf in mirrored glass and spangled vinyl, accessorized with babes, Babycham, and 1950s poodles.

The Jungle Room – the King's lair at Graceland in Memphis, Tennessee – was Presley's interpretation of the tacky-Tiki Polynesian style.

A squadron of flying ducks wings past a collection of Elvis imagery, black memorabilia, cats, cacti, and assorted holiday souvenirs, loaded onto a decorative black Formica sideboard.

and large), designed to soar across wallpapered chimney breasts in the semi-detached homes of middle England, first appeared in the 1930s.

They were inspired perhaps by the hunting-shooting crowd, but they belonged to suburbia's inherent longing for lost countryside (the suburban housing boom of the inter-war years monopolized huge areas of green-belt land). Early originals were made of china or porcelain, often hand-painted, and were produced by a number of potteries including Poole, Beswick, and SylvaC, and the Czechoslovakian company Royal Dux. Some were produced in groups of

five or eight ducks, and brass sets were available. Wall-mounted flying ducks were still commonplace in the 1950s, but in a mass-produced form, often made of cheap plaster, and more readily associated with working-class homes. Indeed, a set of three flew across Hilda Ogden's living-room wall in the classic British television soap opera *Coronation Street*.

As a modern metaphor for low-brow decor, flying ducks have been playfully reproduced in a variety of forms, from flying Batmans to bears and birds of all shapes and sizes, including traditional English ducks. Of interest to collectors are the sets of three Guinness toucans designed to fly across the walls of public houses, carrying tiny pints of beer on their china bills.

Elvis

Singer Elvis Presley, born Tupelo, Mississippi, 1935, died Memphis, Tennessee, 1977. Also known as "Elvis the Pelvis", "The King", and father of the Graceland tourist phenomenon.

Apologies to fans of one of the world's best-loved and most mythologized vocal artists in rock and pop history, but Elvis has to take some of the blame (or credit) for his kitsch status. Those rhinestoned Las Vegas pant-suits, the cheesey movies (*Blue Hawaii, Paradise Hawaiian Style*), the greased quiff, and the bad diet (fried peanut-butter sandwiches?) showed a reckless disregard for good taste.

And as for Graceland – well, Elvis Presley Enterprises have toned down the decor since the King first furnished his 23-room palace in 1957, but his favourite hang-out, the Jungle Room,

☞ *The Three Wahines,* by Tiki-inspired contemporary American artist Josh Agle – better known to his worldwide fans as "Shag".

remains a tacky tribute to Polynesian Pop (highlights include a water feature cascading down a mock rockface, an ice-cream bar, carved Tiki thrones, and green shag pile).

Contrary to popular modern myth, Elvis is not alive and well and living in Michigan (or anywhere else), but he has been immortalized by a vast legacy of Elvis memorabilia and enough impersonators to populate a small planet.

Witco

Acronym for the Washington International Trading Company; the "world's largest chainsaw carving company", founded by William Westenhaver, 1962. "Hand-carved, crafted wood, tempered by fire and polished glowing smooth ... [Witco] speaks out strongly to be investigated," wrote William

Westenhaver in an early brochure promoting the products of his Seattle-based furniture enterprise. Witco decor certainly stood out, but the "immediately interesting and unusual atmosphere" he attributed to his chunky, chainsawn conversation pieces was an acquired taste (acquired, that is, by the minority).

Designed to appeal primarily to the Tiki market, Witco consisted of whole-grain timber, burnished with a torch and crudely whittled into cocktail tables, wall-mounted reliefs (masks, guitars, cats, ships, etc), bedroom sets, fur-fabric sofas (from Bengal tiger to burnt orange and red chin-chin), and Kaü "contemporary idols".

As well as Tiki ranges (such as "African Swag" and "Safari"), the company ventured into curious Conquistador, quasi-Hispanic, medieval heraldic, and Aztec styles. At the height of its success, customers included Hugh Hefner and Elvis (who bought items for his Jungle Room). Latterly it is bought by collectors of the retro Tiki style, though usually it's the sheer awfulness of Witco that appeals.

Tiki

Cult of Polynesian Pop, prevalent among American suburban primitives of the 1950s–'60s; tropical fantasy world of pseudo-Oceanic culture. The Tiki style, a mélange of simulated Pacific-island life, evolved as a generation of thematic bars and supper-clubs in 1950s America. The basic idea was to create a recreational environment in which tribes of suburban escapists could play at being savages in a quasi-tropical atmosphere. Going native, according to the Tiki edict, meant

☞ "Marco Polo furniture group", including dragon-armed sofa with spotted fur upholstery, by 1960s chainsaw carving specialist Witco (the Washington International Trading Company).

The modern "urban archaeologist" displays his collection of vintage Tiki-bar mugs and other vessels in an appropriately tropical setting, furnished with bamboo and palm trees.

wearing flower garlands and aloha shirts, dining on luau pig feasts washed down with extravagantly garnished rum-based cocktails (Pi Yi, Mai Tai, Coffee Grog, Zombie, and others), served up by hula girls to the beat of Hawaiian music.

The decor was a jungle of tropical palms, furnished à la Polynesia with outrigger canoes, Tiki torches, bamboo, totems, exotic masks, and beachcomber lamps. Central to the theme was the "Tiki" itself: a carved idol, best described as a phallus with a face, its form graced everything on the Tiki menu from ceramic cocktail mugs to enormous outdoor effigies guarding the urban temple gates.

Paradise, Tiki-style, first emerged in Los Angeles in the 1930s–'40s with the founding of Don the Beachcomber and Trader Vic's (both of which developed into chains of Tiki

A hula-girl table fountain (complete with lagoon of plastic lilies) forms a mini-South Sea island in a sea of 1950s Formica.

supper-clubs); it took off in the 1950s, and reached fever pitch in the early 1960s, as a proliferation of Luau lounges and Kon-Tiki bars rolled out across urban America. By the 1960s there were Tiki fast-food franchises, motels, "bou-tikis", apartment blocks, and homeware ranges. The demand for bamboo bars, backyard Tiki huts, and tribal art fuelled booming Tiki-related craft industries.

Sadly, the allure of the native night out began to fade in the 1970s, and, though a few classic bars survive, Tiki is a vanishing cultural phenomenon. However, a revival of interest has resulted in a rising tide of "urban archaeologists", or Tiki-enthusiasts, determined to rediscover the lost Oceanic fantasylands of the past.

Vintage art and artifacts provide fascinating insights into the golden age of Polynesian Pop, its vocabulary of Pacific-island clichés, and its pagan rituals and idioms – all of which have inspired new generations of Tiki-themed bars and a resurgence of Tiki art and decoration.

Hula Girl

Pacific-island native, transmogrified as hip-wiggling Goddess of Tiki cult; aka Eve in the Paradise of Polynesian Pop.

Since explorers discovered the exotic Oceanic cultures of the Pacific, the native girls, or *wahines*, of the South Sea islands (Tahiti, Hawaii) have been idolized as icons of universal beauty. "On the isle of Otaheite, where love is the principal occupation," wrote Joseph Banks, a naturalist on Captain Cook's ship *Endeavour*; "... the bodies and souls of the women are formed to perfection."

This global snow-dome collection includes souvenirs from all climates, including snowy New York and sunny Florida.

the wiggling, wobbling, nodding action of the spring-loaded, hula-girl dashboard accessory, or the temptress on top of the television.

Snowdomes

Small scenic blizzard contained in bubble of clear liquid; also known as snowstorms, sno-globes, snow-shakers, snowballs, and, in German, schneekugela.

Dating from the late 19th century, snowdomes are the indirect descendants of Venetian glass paperweights; they first emerged as rare, expensive souvenirs commemorating landmark events such as the inauguration of the Eiffel Tower in Paris in 1889. They re-emerged in the 1920s as mementoes of religious pilgrimages, but it was not until the 1940s, when plastic technology made them cheap to produce, that they really began to conquer the globe as mass-market holiday souvenirs.

American companies Atlas Crystal Works (from 1941) and Enesco (from 1958), and French company Convert (from 1969), established the blueprint for the classic snowdome: a hand-size bubble of clear plastic, encapsulating figures, buildings, or tourist destinations, and tiny flakes of fake snow suspended in distilled water and glycerine.

Snowdome subjects, then as now, range from the religious (saints, crucifixions, popes) to the celebrated (Elvis, Santa Claus, Michelangelo's *David*), but the most common form is the been-there-done-it 3D postcard of, say, the Statue of Liberty, Niagara Falls, or flamingos on a Florida beach. The unlikely combination of snowflakes

The effect of the so-called hula girl on the male species is the stuff of legend: sailors have deserted ships for her, and soldiers have died for her (as in smitten Lt Cable in the 1958 movie *South Pacific*). Now, stereotyped as a topless, grass-skirted diva (complete with exotic garlands and ukulele), she has been reduced to

Edgar Leeteg

The so-called "American Gauguin" (born St Louis, 1904) fathered the art of painting on velvet. Died Tahiti, 1953, leaving 1,700 portraits of nubile native girls and a mansion called Villa Velour.

Edgar Leeteg was working as a billboard-painter and signwriter in California when he left for Tahiti in the 1930s. There he scraped a living by selling erotic paintings of Tahitian beauties to passing sailors for a few dollars. He was then discovered by Barney Davis, a tattooed former submariner turned Honolulu gallery-owner, who dubbed his protégé "the American Gauguin". By the mid-1940s an original Leeteg (topless Micronesian women and other exotic flowers painted on plush black velveteen) could fetch thousands of dollars. Wealth bought the artist a pink Tahitian home called Villa Velour, with an Italian marble summerhouse and an aquarium bar, four marriages, and a hard-drinking, womanizing lifestyle that ended with a fatal motorcycle crash. The works of Leeteg slipped into obscurity, but thanks to the Museum of Velvet Painting, founded in Seattle in 1993, a 21st-century revival is underway.

Liberace

Wladziu Valentino Liberace (1919–87); camp pianist best known for his wardrobe of sensational costumes; also known as "Mr Showmanship".

No doubt his musical skills made a contribution, but it was Liberace's superior talent for self-promotion that made him the richest pianist in history – and he certainly knew how to spend money. On stage he sparkled and shimmered in glitzy ensembles trimmed with sequins, rhinestones, furs, and jewels ("Why don't I slip into something more spectacular" was one of his catchphrases); but he was equally extravagant in the field of home decoration.

In his 1960s–'70s heyday Liberace owned eight homes (in Hollywood, Palm Springs, Las Vegas, and Malibu), all richly furnished with gold, crystal, and marble, as well as the trademark candelabras and pianos, including a piano-shaped swimming pool). The interior of his Hollywood Hills penthouse, for example, was inspired by a combination of styles,

Surrounded by the jewelled extravagance of his Las Vegas mansion, Liberace takes a bubble bath in a $55,000 marble tub.

Examples include studio tableaux of teddies on toyland beaches, saucy postcards (cartoons laden with sexual innuendo), 3D pictures of, say, the Pope, 2D pictures of flamenco dancers (with real fabric skirts), and 1950s-style pictorial collages (of Florida, for example, or Skegness). In postcards, at least, the world knows no bounds.

Flamingos

Tropical lake-wader; sole member of the phoenicopteridae *family; reborn in 1957 as* phoenicopteris ruber plasticus, *a pink flamingo garden ornament (aka "lawn mingo") by Union Products.*

If the flamingo's plumage had been white instead of wild shades of coral and candy pink, this graceful tropical wader would not perhaps have seen its image so flagrantly reproduced in the guise of plastic foodpicks, foam-insulated

including Louis XV, Baroque, Rococo, Regency, and Art Nouveau. Remnants of his estate, exhibited in the Liberace Museum in Las Vegas, include a King Neptune costume encrusted with seashells, a 1934 roadster car covered in Austrian rhinestones, and a platinum candelabra ring with diamond flames.

Holiday Postcards

Pictorial images conveying greetings from abroad.
The whimsical, wish-you-were-here postcard, in its multitude of forms, is too varied a thing to be defined as iconographic, but it is included here to represent the holiday experience, and its associated trade in ersatz souvenirs.

Alongside a recent upsurge of so-called "boring postcards" (e.g. pictures of motorway cafés), the traditional postcard (as in landscapes in 19th-century sepia) has extended to encompass cards of a humorously kitsch or ironic nature.

A sunlit study of teddy bears on a seaside holiday in toyland, by British postcard specialist John Hinde.

can-coolers, or "Flirtin' Flamingo" nylon windsocks. The 21st-century boom in flamingo-related novelties dates back to 1957, when classically trained artist Don Featherstone carved the prototype of a durable plastic lawn flamingo for Union Products in Massachussetts ("thereby making affordable bad taste accessible to the American public"). Over 20 million Featherstone 'mingos have since been sold, and, though widely copied, the "original, world-famous" model is still in production (along with numerous related spin-offs, such as tasteful white "Snomingos"). Its 40th anniversary was celebrated with a book, *Splendour on the Grass* (Schiffer, 1997), for which hundreds of flamingo-loving Americans submitted photographs of their own *phoenicopteris ruber plasticus* in humorous poses and bizarre settings.

Fantastic Plastic

Resinous material that can be moulded into any permanent shape; generic term for man-made polymers (nylon, melamine, polyvinyl, polyethylene, etc).

Ah, plastic. Where would kitsch be without it? This moulded, waterproof substance may be a product of science, but it is central to the art of imitation, as well as the manufacture of the cheap souvenir. The road to fake flowers and fun picnicware was preluded by numerous inventions: from Alexander Parkes' cellulose-based Parkesine (first seen in 1862), and John Wesley Hyatt's thermoplastic Celluloid (1866), to Leo Baekeland's resinous Bakelite (1907). But the most significant landmarks in its history took place in the 1930s with the discoveries of polyvinyl chloride (or PVC), from which vinyl upholstery is made, and polyethylene, now the most common of volume plastics. The word is often used as a pejorative (to mean synthetic, or mass-produced), but the fantastic versatility of plastic has made it the world's most used material.

Viva España! Photographic postcard of Spanish flamenco dancers, stitched with real fabric frills.

Nothing defines kitsch more graphically than leopard spots and fake fur, seen here among the wildlife of the suburban jungle, where a ceramic big cat stalks a herd of flocked plastic deer.

Jungle Prints

Prey of the urban hunter-decorator (simulated pelts of zebra, tiger, leopard, ocelot, etc); raw material of the Out-of-Africa look.

Reproducing the coats of endangered jungle predators in tame polyester is the ultimate in frivolous kitsch. Synthetic big-cat skins also convey an element of glamour (as in man-killing leopard-spotted lingerie); but the enduring allure of tiger-print velour has a complex history, rooted in the genuinely tasteless fur trade.

Early examples of fur furnishings include tigerskin rugs and other trophies of the "great white hunters", who stalked the jungles of colonial India and Africa, shooting beasts for sport. The high value of pelts turned game hunting into an industry; and by 1962 (when Jackie Kennedy made a public appearance in fetching leopardskin), the international trade in exotic furs was worth around $30 million. Marketed as a luxury fashion accessory ("untamed, provocatively dangerous ... bringing out the animal instinct in you"), they were very expensive; hence the fake-fur finishes popularized in the 1950s were the cheap copy-cats of an elite aspiration.

Following the "Save the Tiger" campaign, launched in 1969, the fur trade went into decline. Not so the fake-fur trade, which now provides the only respectable way of living with leopardskin. Kitsch, maybe, but not distasteful.

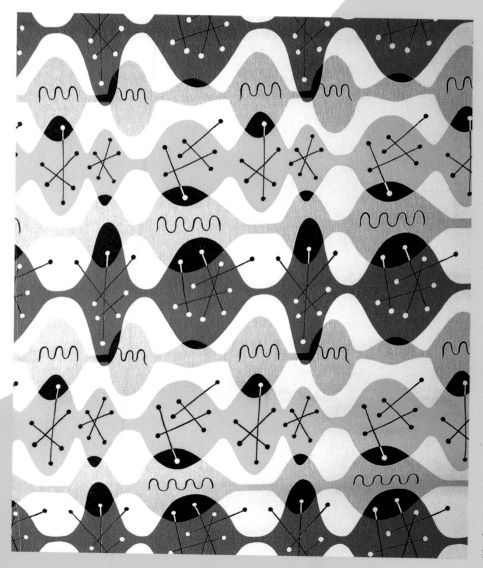

Atomic Age abstract, featuring amoebic shapes of bright colour, in a 1954 textile design, "Hourglass", by W. Hertzberger.

Fifties Fabrics

Expressions of post-war joie de vivre *by Lucienne Day and other luminaries of the 1951 Festival of Britain style.*

After years of Utility goods and dreary wartime khaki, Britain's textiles came out in a gay show of exuberant colour and splashy designs. Collectors' items of the period include the Miro-inspired "Calyx" (for the Festival of Britain, 1951), and "Herb Anthony" (Heals, 1954), both designed by Lucienne Day; "Hourglass" (a bright red-yellow-black, atomic-amoebic abstract) by W. Hertzberger for Turnbull and Stockdale (1954); and "Vibration", designed by Nicola Wood for Heals (1960). Now treated like works of art, stretched onto frames like canvases, these are among the Rembrandts of the 1950s aesthetic. Less valuable, and more kitsch, are the largely unattributed vintage prints designed for kitchens (fruit, vegetables, cooking utensils, etc) and bathrooms (floating bubbles, toothbrushes, shaving sticks, and tropical fish swimming across diaphanous plastic).

Formica

American brand name, founded 1913, applied as generic to describe plastic laminates used in industry and home furnishings; close family relatives include Warerite (Swedish) and Abet Laminati (Italian). Formica's enduring association with 1950s diners, drive-ins, and spike-legged dinette tables would not be enough to justify a place in the world of kitsch. Indeed, Formica's pre-war industrial heritage is not the least bit whimsical. So what

☞ Grotto decor: baroque seashell mosaic in an urban bathroom, by muralist Brian Lewis (*see* pages 92–95).

is it doing here? Well, that's down to a genius for faking almost anything, from woodgrains and metals to floral textiles. What other material can provide a hygienic, easy-clean surface decorated with lace, glitter, pebbledash, or pictures of ballerinas?

Pioneered by two young engineers, Herbert Faber and Daniel O'Conor, the material was first produced in 1910 at the Westinghouse Electric and Manufacturing Company in Pittsburgh. Initially, it consisted of sheets of canvas or paper impregnated with Bakelite,

and was first used as a component of cars, aircraft, and military radio sets. In the 1930s Formica moved into decorative finishes with a revamped manufacturing process that, in essence, still survives: layers of printed craft paper, soaked in melamine resins, and sandwiched into thin, rigid sheets. Early Formica furnished the interiors of cruise ships, Union Pacific railroad coaches, and office lobbies, but finishes were limited to black, pearl, linen, and woodgrain.

The Formica brand name hit the British market in 1947, just before the new post-war breed of plastic laminates led a home-front revolution. "Life with Formica is bliss" sang the adverts, which advocated a new age of liberating, wipe-clean kitchens in dozens of designs and "jewel-bright" colours. In those days you could buy a sheet of the stuff and turn an ordinary table into a "thing of beauty". However, the DIY boom proved detrimental to Formica's image, and the company gradually withdrew from the consumer market.

Plastic laminates found new respectability when the Italian design group Memphis applied them liberally to a collection of post-modern furniture shown at the Milan Furniture Fair in 1981. But Formica's golden age still belongs to the 1950s – the age of the free-form coffee tables and vanitory units clad in Luxwood, which are now considered retro classics.

Shell Art

Plundered treasures of the seashore, utilized in various forms of rococo decoration; not to be confused with eggshell art.

Nature sometimes brings out the worst in us. How else does one explain the inclination to fashion small objects (mice, for example) from seashells and glue? Indeed, it doesn't matter where you are in the world-on-sea, there is a shell shop somewhere serving up curtains of shells-on-strings or, indeed, mice with shell ears.

Even the most noble forms of shell art err on the side of kitsch. For example, the subterranean garden grottos popular in 18th-century landscaped gardens were encrusted with exotic shells pirated from the South Seas (plus camp figures of Neptune, waterfalls, and glittering walls of quartz and abalone). This tradition (popular with obsessive 20th-century "outsider" artists) is continued in modern rococo mosaics, formed from shells (cockles, mussels, oysters, etc), in suburban gardens (and bathrooms).

Painting by Number

Popular paint kits, created in the 1950s by Palmer Paint Company, Detroit, under Craft Master logo.

The "Painting by Number" kit-art phenomenon, born in America in 1951, was the brainchild of Max Klein (owner of the Palmer Paint Company)

☞ Big-eyed painting-by-number portrait by Walter Keane, and a matching cat by the artist known as Gig.

☞ Since she was born in 1959, Barbie, the all-American super-doll, has become one of the world's best-selling toys.

figurative studies, or forms of narrative realism such as matadors, Indian chiefs, dogs, kittens, autumn foliage, and mountain scenery, as well as masterpieces like the *Last Supper*. Painters in Europe, meanwhile, preferred cottages and Parisian street scenes; but, whatever the subject, they all bore the distinctive jigsaw-like appearance of a Craft Master original. Despite the millions of Painting by Number works of art in circulation, well-executed vintage examples are now becoming collectable. Much cheaper than a Rembrandt, too.

Barbie®

All-American fashion queen, born New York Toy Fair, 1959; conceived by Mattel founders Ruth and Elliott Handler; named after daughter Barbara. One of the world's best-selling toys. An eleven-and-a-half-inch vinyl "uber-babe" with an impossibly perfect figure and big hair, Barbie's international superstardom has made her one of the most familiar faces on the planet. Since her first appearance in a candy-striped sunsuit, the ultimate material girl has modelled a vast wardrobe of outfits designed by, among others, Christian Dior, Yves Saint-Laurent, Donna Karan, and Karl Lagerfeld. She has dressed up as everyone from biker Barbie to Bond Girl.

Accessories include boyfriend Ken ("he's a doll") launched in 1961, little sister Skipper (1964), horses called Dallas and Midnight, a Starlight Motor Home, a sports car, several pink-lilac homes, and more pairs of shoes than Imelda Marcos. And, despite being berated by feminists as an unsuitable role model,

and artist Dan Robbins. Marketed under the Craft Master logo, with a promise that "every man is a Rembrandt", each kit consisted of two paintbrushes, numbered pre-mixed paints, and a pre-drawn canvas mapped with corresponding numbered spaces ready to be coloured in by the artist. The idea was reviled by critics as a "violation of art", but the public embraced the concept with enthusiasm. What started out as a popular hobby soon became a craze, as 12 million kits were sold in the first three years.

Although abstract art was represented in the range of kits available, the amateur artists (or "number filler-inners") tended to prefer

Barbie has survived over 40 years of cosmetic reconstructions and dazzling costume changes to remain the princess of her own pretty-in-pink, plastic dream world.

Monalisiana

Art of trivializing Renaissance masterpiece; as in Mona Lisa *merchandising, courtesy of Leonardo da Vinci.*

The essence of Monalisiana is in putting a proverbial moustache on the most familiar of Renaissance masterpieces, by presenting its image in the form of amusing merchandise. Classic examples include *Mona Lisa* socks, shower curtains, clocks, or "Giggling *Mona Lisa* pillows". Monalisiana encapsulates new art as well as artifacts: for example, a flatulent cartoon *Mona Lisa* (Steve Best, 1992) captioned "Mona was trying not to smile as she waited for her silent fart to reach Leonardo"; or *Mona Pigga* (1986), modelled by Miss Piggy for the Jim Henson Studio's Kermitage Collection. Loosely speaking, Monalisiana also relates to the trivialization of other Old Masters (such as the *Last Supper*, or Michelangelo's *David*).

Dolly Parton

Diminutive, big-busted country singer, born Tennessee, 1946; founder of Smoky Mountain theme park Dollywood.

Heroine of a real-life, rags-to-riches country ballad, Dolly Parton describes herself as "totally artificial on the outside, and totally genu-wine on the inside" – a state she achieved by way of numerous cosmetic nips and tucks, a collection of elaborate high-rise wigs (when asked how long it takes to do her hair, she replies: "I don't know, I'm never there"), and a taste for loud, larger-than-life costumes erring on the side of pink frothy frocks, decorated denim, and cowboy fringes. Dolly enhanced her status as a kitsch icon by opening Dollywood, a Smoky Mountain music theme park, at Pigeon Forge in her native Tennessee, next door to sister attraction Dolly's Splash Country.

Playboy

Casino-club empire founded in 1960s by purveyor of soft porn Hugh Hefner (born 1926), creator of Playboy *and the "Bunny Girl".*

The Playboy empire is best known for the armies of beautiful "bunny girls" created by Hugh Hefner to serve Martinis and sex-appeal to club clients. Having to wear bow-ties, rabbit ears, and fluffy cottontails attached to the rear-ends of skimpy satin bunny suits might seem ludicrously undignified, but the allure of becoming glamorous icons has always attracted high-class girls to bunnydom, particularly in the 1960s. Behind the scenes, "Hef", the ultimate playboy himself, cultivated an image of the sophisticated bachelor lounge-lizard, partying at his millionaire mansion in a red-silk dressing gown, surrounded by a bevy of "playmates". Vintage Playboy collectables include black-glass ashtrays, cigarette lighters, and pens, all bearing the club's famous monochrome bunny motif.

The irrepressible Dolly Parton dresses up bunny-girl-style for the cover of *Playboy* magazine.

Kitsch
Spaces

☞ Dusk at the Shady Dell auto park, where lamps glow through Polynesian-print drapes in trailer windows, and strings of party lights shimmer against shiny aluminium coach-work.

☜ Ed Smith and Rita Personett in a 1949 Airstream, one of their collection of seven restored vintage travel trailers.

Auto Magic

Ed Smith and Rita Personett never meant to run a trailer park. When they bought the Shady Dell in 1995, the rundown auto camp was simply intended as a place to park their personal collection of vintage aluminium travel trailers. However, as their collection grew they began to wonder whether they might rent these beautifully restored vehicles to overnight guests. So they gave up their careers in antique dealing, and turned the Shady Dell into "a living museum of the bygone days of trailering".

On the fringe of Old Bisbee, a mile-high mining town in southern Arizona's Mule Mountains, the Shady Dell started life in 1927, offering camping pitches and "pull-thru" spaces for trailer traffic passing through on Highway 80 (which runs from San Diego, California, to Savannah, Georgia). By the time Ed and Rita came along nearly 70 years later, the place had "hit the skids", but its provenance and authentic retro ambience made it the perfect home for a 1952 "home-made", a 1954 Crown, and a bullet-shaped El Rey, circa 1957.

A classic 1949 Airstream, and three 1950s park-home models (a Spartan Manor, a Spartanette, and a Royal Mansion), were soon added to the collection. The varnished birchwood and polished aluminium interiors were restored to pristine condition, and, to add to their charm,

Ed and Rita decorated and furnished each trailer in appropriate period style. The refrigerators, the drapes, the coffee percolators, the magazines, and even the cutlery, are all vintage originals. Ed confesses to cheating on the heating, the radios, and the swamp coolers, but even these modern appliances have been chosen to look the part. Hence, a night in a Shady Dell trailer is like stepping into a 1950s timewarp.

The decor in the 1951 Royal Mansion is Ed's tribute to the neighbours he grew up with in Concord, California – Bill and Edna Maples, and their son Bobby. "My mother and father decorated their brand-new house with Early American furniture and drove a Chevy Station Wagon," recalls Ed. "The Maples, however, had a boomerang coffee table, leopard-print-covered couch, and a rattan bar where they served Martinis. They listened to Jerry Lee Lewis and Elvis, and drove a red convertible. Somehow life seemed more fun at the Maples'."

☞ The Mansion trailer has an original 1950s television, complete with modern video player and copies of old black-and-white B-movies, such as *The Creature from the Black Lagoon*.

☜ The 1951 Royal Mansion park-home model trailer is kitted out with vintage Martini glasses, swizzle sticks, and cocktail shaker.

☞ Romantic two-somes can sleep beneath mirror-finish polished aluminium, under brightly coloured chenille, in the 1949 Airstream.

The Royal Mansion is furnished with a breakfast booth in green vinylette and immaculate yellow laminate. A leopardskin-print carpet in the lounge area adds to the exotic feel. Guests can play a selection of old records (choose from *Doowop Classics*, Louis Jordan, or *Under Hawaii Skies*) on a vintage Symphonic phonograph, and watch black-and-white movies on an original Setchell Carlson TV (wired to a modern video recorder, hidden behind a jungle-print drape). Martini glasses and a shaker are provided.

In the Airstream the theme is romance (with pink flamingos, albums of 1950s wedding photographs, and colourful bedroom chenille). The little "homemade" (a compact ten-foot model made by a DIY enthusiast from a plan out of *Popular Mechanics*) is furnished in vintage Southwestern style: a mix of Mexican kitsch, cacti, and bright, sunny colours.

The Shady Dell is also home to a restored 1957 diner (a Valentine ten-stool model, complete with red vinyl and neon), an early 1960s Flxible airport bus, and a Chris Craft yacht. Found in a boatyard on the Sacramento Delta in California, this 38-foot pleasure boat was a wreck before she was transported to Bisbee for restoration and decoration, and renamed the *Rita D*.

Previous page

The cosy ten-foot "homemade", made by a trailer enthusiast in 1952, is lined with varnished birchwood cabinetry, and decorated in a kitschy, Mexico-in-America, Southwestern style.

⌦ Model ships, miniature sailors, and copies of *Motor Boating* magazine are some of the nautical accessories on the *Rita D*.

The Chris Craft yacht, a 38-foot pleasure boat moored in a thicket of pampas and bamboo, is decked out with leopardskin and jungle prints, comfortable dry-land furniture, and ship-shaped memorabilia.

Now, docked on dry land beneath a custom-built shelter to protect her from the desert heat, the *Rita D* offers a chance to be the captain of the ship without getting seasick. Done up like a mini-gin palace, it has a stern-end, sit-out area shaded by pampas grass and bamboo, a galley kitchen, and a comfortable living room – all lined with polished wood and chrome, and decked out with vintage boating memorabilia (anchor-motif kitchenware, ship-shaped lamps, and sea-creature towels).

Ed and Rita are always dreaming up new ideas for 1950s-themed interiors, such as a Polynesian-island makeover destined for the Flxible bus. "Ed reckons we are just frustrated decorators," says Rita. "All we really want to do is travel around the country buying cute things and then find some place to put them. The fun part of owning travel trailers is dressing them up."

Every Formica surface is crowded with 1950s kitsch, including miniature flamenco dancers, black memorabilia, and wireware from the Festival of Britain era.

Billy and Lily sit at a chrome-trimmed spike-legged table, in a kitchen-diner furnished with a blue-painted "Del Boy" cabinet, red-plastic fake flowers, and a Hula-girl table fountain.

Kitsch Deluxe

Lucie Smailes' house is an ordinary two-up-two-down in suburbia, except that the interior appears to have got lost in time somewhere around 1955. Almost everything she owns, from furnishing fabric and flamenco dolls to clothing, and even clothes pegs, is an original from the period – but there is no sign of Charles and Ray Eames, or Robin and Lucienne Day. Lucie eschews the finer end of collectable 1950s furniture, and shops for early examples of mass-produced chain-store goods from the golden age of kitsch. However, what she has created is not exactly a timewarp: the true post-war home would not have been so vividly colourful, nor stuffed with so many things.

Set against a basic colour palette of custard, bubblegum, and candyfloss, Lucie's kitchen furnishings include a classic yellow dinette table and matching spike-leg chairs, an original 1950s refrigerator (in spray-on lipstick pink), and one of those painted tallboy cabinets, once a common feature of working-class homes, and known, these days, as a "Del Boy" cupboard (after the kitchen of the character Derek Trotter, on the set of British comedy *Only Fools and Horses*).

Every Formica surface is crowded with flamenco dancers, Festival of Britain-era wireware (with cocktail-cherry feet), illuminated posies of fake roses ("I love roses," she says), fairy lights, and framed glamour-girl prints by Tretchikoff, Lynch, and other masters of the Woolworths school of art. Lucie's idea of a snack? A handful of jelly beans dispensed from a slot machine, and served on red-and-white-spotted picnicware. However, she admits that her two children, Billy and Lily, would prefer to live in a "normal" house.

The 1950s living-room furniture includes a ship-shaped cocktail cabinet (complete with cocktail paraphernalia), a red vinylette sofa, and a glitzy mirrored-glass display case stuffed with plastic flower paperweights. There's also a plastic budgie in a chrome cage, strings of Chinese lanterns hanging from the ceiling, and a pair of post-war drapes in fun boat-print fabric (the window-wear equivalent of a Hawaiian shirt).

Lucie's fantasy interpretation of the 1950s home is, she agrees, a form of escapism: a journey into a nostalgic world of cocktail hours and exotic package holidays, rock'n'roll and ra-ra skirts. "To me, it's a form of anti-depressant," she says. "It makes me smile."

☞ Lucie Smailes' mind-boggling collection of chainstore kitsch includes colourful paper lanterns, a boat-shaped cocktail bar, and a pair of period Hawaiian-style curtains, and even runs to a wardrobe of 1950s clothes.

☜ Framed glamour-girl print, *Red Ribbon Girl*, by Lou Shabney, with a garland of flower lights.

Overleaf
Fairy-frocked Lily investigates a cool candy-pink refrigerator. The plastic beaded curtain is modern, but the "Homemaker" plates are originals designed for Woolworths by Enid Seeney in 1955.

☜ Jungle-green walls
set off a collection of
Tiki mugs and lamps,
a Chinese lantern, a
vintage B-movie poster,
and a sunset over
the South Seas.

Little Polynesia

When Brandi Kvetko and Chris Swanberg moved into their 1947 house they discovered a wall of original wallpaper hidden under a layer of panelling – and they couldn't have been more excited if they had been a couple of archaeologists discovering the ruins of a lost city. The Polynesian-style wallpaper was carefully exposed, and, teamed up with jungle-green paintwork, provides the perfect backdrop for the Tiki-moderne decor for which the couple share a passion.

They also collect vintage slot cars, B-movie memorabilia, Rat Fink monsters, cat kitsch, and wacky lamps, but their favourite things reflect their taste for the whimsical cult of Polynesian Pop, encompassing tropical bamboo, 1950s urban-American Tiki, and primitive Witco furniture. The chainsaw-carved Witco, of which Brandi has a small collection, includes a "Log Kitty", a crazy guitar, and a pair of crudely carved bar stools with leatherette seats. "We are pining for a Witco bar to match," says Brandi, but the couple already have a bar. Loaded with Tiki cocktail mugs, and flanked by a pair of hammered-copper pictures of exotic dancers, it shares living-room space with a 1950s amoebic coffee table, a hula-girl lamp (with "bulby" light-up boobs), and Ivan, the eight-foot Tiki totem. Designed originally to preside over suburban outdoor rituals, such as Tiki barbecues, Ivan was a column of blackened timber until he was transformed with jungle-green paint into the ideal companion for the Polynesian wallpaper.

☞ These curious,
but highly collectable,
burnished-wood bar
stools are part of
Brandi's collection of
1950s chainsaw-carved
furniture by Witco.

Overleaf
Original 1950s Polynesian-
style wallpaper provides
the perfect setting for an
urban-American Tiki bar,
bamboo furniture, and
an eight-foot indoor
Tiki-totem called Ivan.

Dale Sizer's Tiki-diner kitchen is equipped with an original 1950s refrigerator and matching vintage oven, accessorized with masks, mugs, and retro advertising, and decorated with checked sticky-back plastic.

Tiki Palace

Dale Sizer's long fascination with the American-Polynesian Tiki style began with a television show, *Adventures in Paradise* (1959–62), in which the hero, Adam Troy, sailed around the South Pacific islands in a schooner called the *Tiki*. To the young Dale, tales of the rebellious Troy, with his pagan totems and Tahitian women, provided the perfect escape from the "crucifixes and cold weather" of his Catholic upbringing in Washington State.

Now an artist and animation illustrator, Dale has turned his retro apartment in West Hollywood into a tropical-island dream world, crowded with the primitive carvings and reproduction native art that once furnished the Tiki-themed cocktail bars and motels of post-war California. His blue fishnet ball lamp, for example, came from the former Kelbo's restaurant in Los Angeles. The double-height volume has been divided by inserting a palette-shaped mezzanine floor that houses Dale's studio. To play up the Tiki ambience, he has lined the walls with split bamboo, added leopard and tigerskin prints, and installed a collection of vintage furniture. His dedication to the 1950s lifestyle even runs to owning original kitchen appliances, and watching old movies on a reproduction 1958 television.

 With its mood lighting, South-Sea-island carvings, jungle prints, bamboo, and exotic pin-ups, the living space has the ambience of a 1950s Tiki nightclub. The television in the corner is a copy of a 1958 model called the Philco Predicta.

☞ The dining room is a mix of junk-shop furniture covered in paint, or paint-splodged fabric, and finer pieces like an antique glass chandelier, and a 1930s standard lamp.

☜ Mary Rose Young's exuberant decorating style extends to hand-painted doors, with rose-shaped ceramic door furniture.

English Rose

There is a farmhouse-style kitchen with a Welsh dresser, beams, bare-board floors, cats, and a couple of outhouses, but thereafter nothing about Mary Rose Young's home conforms to the traditional image of a country cottage. She and her husband, musician Phil Butcher, have eschewed the clichés of English country living (all whitewash and rustic stripped pine), and decorated their home with patterned paint effects and vibrant colour – all done in the "energetic hand-done look" that characterizes the earthenware pottery that Mary Rose produces in a studio next door. Her uninhibited artwork, from which no surface is excluded, features wiggly stripes, squiggles, spots, checks, and lots of her favourite roses. Instead of roses round the front door, this cottage has hand-painted rose motifs all over the interior walls.

The house (formerly a pair of quarrymen's cottages in Gloucestershire's Forest of Dean) is furnished with a mix of "cheap, rubbishy furniture" and antiques. "It's a bit like a theatre set," says Mary Rose. "So it needs a few, nice expensive things to give it a bit of authority." In the dining room, a junk-shop table, coated with bright gloss paint, is lit by a Victorian glass chandelier.

Overleaf left:
Malcolm, one of three house cats, settles on the blue bed. This primary-coloured medieval-style bedroom has a tented muslin ceiling, and an ornate ceramic basin.

Overleaf right:
A spiral staircase leads down to the dressing room, or "tent room", furnished with a hand-painted chipboard floor, striped canvas cupboards, and a Buddhist shrine.

In the "marital bedroom", an antique bed is the centrepiece of a bold colour scheme that hints at medieval pageantry. The ceiling is a canopy of yellow muslin and fairy lights trimmed with bunting; in the corner there's a Mary Rose pedestal basin edged with ceramic roses.

There is more pageantry in the dressing room, which features a pair of his-and-hers wardrobes, masquerading as canvas jousting tents, and Phil's Buddhist shrine, housed on an unremarkable 1940s sideboard, jazzed up with red and yellow paint. The spiral staircase was made from tank plate by sculptor John Foster. Many examples of Mary Rose's colour-glazed pottery (sold chiefly to buyers in Germany and the USA) decorate every corner of the house, and also include some personal projects. In the bathroom, for example, a bog-standard porcelain toilet and a wall of ordinary white tiles have been hand-decorated and kiln-fired to produce stripes of coloured enamel, and a wild fishy mural with an underwater marine theme – typical of the pots and potty decor in this atypical country cottage.

Desert Mystery

Set in the foothills of South Mountain Park, Phoenix, Boyce Luther Gulley's Mystery
Castle is one of Arizona's most eccentric tourist attractions. Built of native stone, adobe, and
recycled rubbish, topped by a crazy line of crenellated parapets and a funny little turret, this desert
folly is also the home of Mary Lou Gulley. Her dusty living rooms are a curious mix of scrapyard
furnishings and whimsical Southwestern style (red-silk chilli peppers, patchwork, and cacti ribs, with
accents of saloon bar), but for downright strangeness, nothing beats the castle's mysterious history.

The 18-room Mystery Castle in Arizona was built from stone, adobe, and scrapyard junk by eccentric recluse Boyce Luther Gulley, between 1930 and 1945.

It began in 1927, when Seattle businessman Boyce Luther Gulley left his office for a doctor's appointment and disappeared. His wife and little girl, Mary Lou, never saw or heard from him again. They had no idea what had become of him until they were notified of his death 18 years later. "Daddy Gulley", they learned, had been diagnosed with tuberculosis, and, in fear of infecting his family, had escaped to a reclusive existence in Arizona. There he had settled on South Mountain, and spent his time constructing an elaborate shelter out of anything he could lay his hands on. Gulley's health was clearly restored by the desert climate, because he lived long enough to build the 18-room mansion he left to his abandoned wife and daughter. In Mary Lou's own words, "the little girl, now a middle-aged princess, dwells in her sandcastle, living the last fairytale".

Boasting 13 fireplaces, and a confection of mud and petroglyphs held together by a mortar of cement, calcium, and goat's milk, her father's legacy is ingenious as well as eccentric. An inverted bathtub serves as an exhaust vent; depression-glass dishes form doorway transoms; and there are inventive uses made of automobile parts, bottle glass, and glazed brick-kiln rejects. "My daddy used to call them klinkers; then Frank Lloyd Wright started using them – now they call them expensive."

Typical of Gulley's handiwork is the Cactus Room, a bedroom built around the skeleton of an ancient saguaro cactus (a protected species unique to the Sonoran Desert), featuring a pebble mosaic

A bedroom in the castle is furnished with a curious mix of antiques and kitty kitsch, with accents of Wild West saloon bar.

A statue of St Francis carved by a local Native American boy, stuffed birds, and a distant view of downtown Phoenix in a haze of urban pollution.

A tin-plate desert armadillo adds a dash of bright colour to dusty desert stonework, and cactus-spine chairs.

Overleaf
Some of Mary Lou's housemates (a comic stuffed animal and a stocking-faced rag doll), sitting at a table laid with a rabbit-in-a-dish on a cowhide cloth, make a curious kitchen tableau.

The Cactus Room, Boyce Luther Gulley's bedroom, was built around the skeleton of an emblematic saguaro cactus, using pebbles, car parts, and disused sleepers from the Sante Fe Railroad.

floor, sleepers from the Sante Fe Railroad, and a window spoked with the wheels of a Stutz Bearcat car. To her father's antiques and found objects, Mary Lou has added a personal collection of stuffed animals and birds, rag-work, hand-painted cushions, and kitty kitsch (portraits of her pet cats, Mona Meow and Cleocatra), and dozens of hand-written proverbs and puns. "He who does not like cats was a rat in a former life", she declares in a sign in her "Garden of Weeden".

Despite moments of entertaining insanity – like the kitchen tableau, in which a cartoon creature dines with a stocking-faced rag doll at a table laid with pewter and cowhide – the castle won an Emmy Award in 1999 for its contribution to tourism. Plus, Mary Lou has had the good sense to ensure its future. Under the auspices of the Mystery Castle Foundation, her extraordinary desert home will always remain open to the public.

Electric Palace

It is no surprise to learn that the flamboyant fashion and textile designer Zandra Rhodes is unable to live without colour. Ever since she launched her first solo collection in 1969, thereafter rising to international fame as the Punk Princess of haute couture, colour has been her dictum in everything from fashion to theatrical face-paint. Even if you don't recall her trademark clothes (all jewelled safety-pins, and hand-sewn rips in floaty, screen-printed fabrics), who could forget her hair colour, which over the years has moved through a spectrum of electric shades, from green to candyfloss pink and fire-engine red?

In her lofty penthouse apartment in London, Zandra's love of colour is expressed in a dramatically proportioned living space decorated with vibrant rainbow paintwork. "I started by drawing chalk lines on the floor to delineate stripes of red, orange, green, and yellow," she says.

Zandra Rhodes' rainbow penthouse is striped with hand-painted colour and furnished with bright accessories.

"Then when the stripes were painted, I thought now let's see how they look going up the wall." As vivid as a Rhodes ballgown, the whole ensemble is dressed with accessories – rosettes of fabric pinned like brooches to the walls; swathes of hand-printed fabric and pink Lurex tossed over tables and sofas; and glassy pendant chandeliers sparkling like jewellery in the sunlight that floods through rows of windows. These long windows and a small patio garden offer views of the London skyline and adjacent rooftop penthouses, including the home of writer and British television presenter, Jonathan Meades.

Zandra splits her time between London and a second home in Del Ray, California, but the rainbow penthouse is where her heart lies – not only because it's close to her English roots, but also because it sits right on top of her dream project, the Zandra Rhodes Fashion and Textile Museum: a permanent exhibition space, devoted to the work of inspirational British fashion designers from the latter half of the 20th century to the present day.

The museum's raw material is a converted cash-and-carry warehouse in south London, purchased by Zandra in 1997, and transformed from a bombed-out 1960s relic into a striking

An abstraction of dazzling decor, seen through the glitter of a glass chandelier made for Zandra by sculptor Andrew Logan.

Overleaf
Pink Lurex fabric and electric shades of paint provide the setting for pillars and exotic statues, Z-shaped tables, Indian souvenirs, and contemporary art.

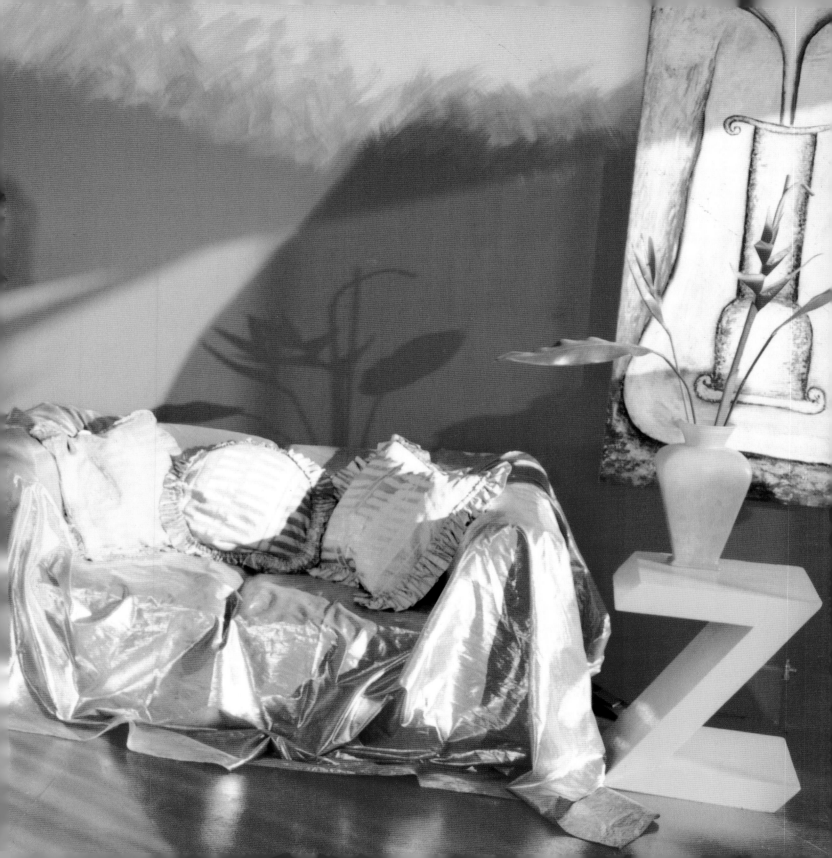

A pair of pink-wigged mannequin models, dressed in Zandra originals, are almost part of the furniture.

The hand-painted roses in Zandra's ultra-pink bedroom spread from the walls onto her customized exercise bike. The carpet was made to her own design, and the painting is by artist and friend Duggie Fields.

landmark building by Mexico's famous modernist architect Ricardo Legorreta (another international designer with a taste for bold colour).

Legorreta's revamped building, his first European project, incorporates a tangerine, hot-pink, and yellow facade, the Grand Pink Foyer, and nine apartments, one of which is Zandra's home. A light, upper-floor duplex, it's a home that often doubles as a fashion showroom, and is occasionally used as a catwalk. Despite its close proximity to the headquarters of its workaholic owner's fashion empire on the floor below, it has the air of an extravagant palace in permanent party mode.

Zandra's multicoloured palace is furnished with a series of exotic papier-mâché figures, like handmaidens at a Nubian court, which were, indeed, made for a party; a collection of lipsticked mannequins, frocked in Rhodes chiffon, stand around in corners looking glamorous; there are souvenirs brought back from India; glitter-swan planters of plastic foliage; old-fashioned tailors' dummies on Z-shaped occasional tables. Many of the paintings and sculptures that decorate the walls are by Zandra's friends – artist Duggie Fields, and glass sculptor Andrew Logan (whose jewelled bust of Zandra was unveiled at London's National Portrait Gallery by the Queen in 1994). The art of decorating a pink-pink bedroom with a splash of hand-painted fuchsia roses is pure, unadulterated Zandra.

Mock Baroque

Muralist and decorative painter Brian Lewis loves the idea of a house "where every room is a surprise, and you can move from one to the other depending on your mood". He is inspired by the tradition of the Grand Tour (in which 18th-century travellers returned from visits to the ancient world with marble columns, classical statues, and wild ideas for shell grottos). His mentor is Ludwig II, the "mad king of Bavaria", who built Germany's "fairytale" castles, Neuschwanstein and Linderhof.

These aspirations would seem beyond the scope of a modestly proportioned, one-bedroom apartment, but Brian has a talent for faking opulence. Using *trompe l'oeil* artistry, gilding, and marbling, shells, paper, papier-mâché, and a few ideas brought back from his global travels, he has created the illusion of a miniature palace. The fruit of his compulsive decorating habit is not, he says, intended to be taken seriously, but enjoyed for what it is: "A dream, a

☞ The Thai Temple bedroom features a home-made four-poster bed crowned with lights, a ceiling of stick-on stars, and two parallel walls of mirrored tiles, reflecting an infinity of fractured images.

☜ The grotto bathroom is a baroque fantasy of shells, mirrored mosaics, plastic foliage, fake wildlife, and painted papier-mâché rocks.

fantasy, an escape from the outside world". In his Thai bedroom, inspired by a visit to south-east Asia, he escapes into an exotic temple of embroidered fabrics, sacred elephants, and the sweet smell of incense. In the bathroom, the fantasy is a faux grotto, complete with plaster rock faces, trailing plastic foliage, shell decorations, and a mirror mosaic floor. A television sits in a craggy recess above the bathtub, and there is a spooky little skeleton fountain that turns on with the lights.

The baroque living room, all *trompe l'oeil* pillars, loggias, statues, and romantic Arcadian landscapes, represents a pictorial album of places he's visited (Salzburg, Istanbul, Prague, Bavaria). Some high-quality furniture includes gilded Napoleonic thrones, alabaster vases, and a black Corinthian rug on a hand-painted floor, but Brian has made good use of his imagination. A few Renaissance-style angels, and lots of tiny pieces of gold card, decorate the original plasterwork; a 19th-century French crystal mirror is jazzed up with brass candlesticks; and who would guess that the crested armoire is a paint-treated wardrobe from Ikea – "the cheapest one they had"? His creations, he admits, are as ephemeral as a stage set – "You are not supposed to look at anything too closely."

☞ The cosmic Space Kitchen is dolled up like an intergalactic space ship. The *Barbarella* mural was painted for Kari by two artist friends.

✍ Dressed in a glitter-pink shift, this disco babe is one of a collection of over 400 Barbie dolls.

Dolly Mixture

The Los Angeles home of performance artist Kari French is devoted to 1960s psychedelia, and the "groovy retro" mod style. "I love mod clothing, decor, music, film, cars – the whole gamut," says Kari. She also loves toys, and has never really grown out of playing with dolls.

An impressive collection includes Betty Boops, Astro Boys, Power Puff girls, Munster dolls, the entire cast of *The Simpsons*, and a fashion parade of over 400 Barbie dolls (including a 1959 original, Space Camp Barbie, Barbie on a Harley, Barbie as Audrey Hepburn, and collectable Cleopatra Barbie). Dolls dangle from ceilings, hang out in display cabinets, and stand around on shelves, as do television- and comic-themed lunch boxes, Thermos flasks, and plastic playthings

from Pick and Save. Using a multitude of cheap toys as a form of wallpaper, explains Kari, is a neat way of covering up damp patches and earthquake damage.

In the Space Kitchen, where Barbie meets *Barbarella*, the night-sky walls and cosmic ceiling are festooned with flying saucers, aliens, space-guns, rocket-shaped fairy lights, *Thunderbirds*, *Wonder Woman* (and other superheroes), and sci-fi movie memorabilia. The room was designed to "resemble the interior of a giant spaceship", though the theme was thrown a little off course when Kari acquired a neon "World's Finer Toys" sign, which usurped her plan to paint a *trompe l'oeil* window looking down on the imaginary planet she was about to land on.

In the bedroom Kari shifts into 1970, with a funky minimalist ensemble loosely based on Rhoda Morgenstern's apartment in *The Mary Tyler Moore Show*. The day-glo colour scheme (pink, purple, magenta, tangerine) was kicked off by a retro shag-pile carpet bought in New York. Kari combines flea-market originals and vintage fabric with a bit of Ikea and ingenuity (she designed the bed herself). It's the perfect place, she says, for dressing up as a "groovy, mod, human Barbie".

Kari's purple-magenta bedroom, inspired by the Mary Tyler Moore sitcom of the 1970s, is furnished with bubbly inflatables, retro fabrics, and shag-pile carpet.

☞ Astronaut Barbie
floats in the upper space
of Kari's sci-fi kitchen,
past the bright lights
of a neon toy-shop sign.

A late-Victorian mantelpiece takes on a bright new look with vivid green paintwork, and a loose arrangement of gift-shop souvenirs, including Elvis candles, fake lilies, and a Chinese flower flask.

A collection of sunburst clocks and mirrors, circa 1930–50, covers a wall of leopard-skin-print wallpaper.

Absolutely Poptastic

Craig Masson and Andrew McMinn describe the ersatz decor of their South London living room as "kitschy colonial", with hints of Rococo, and "very Pierre et Gilles". On one vivid red wall they have mounted a herd of flocked plastic deer heads ("that grand hall look without the taxidermy"); on another they have used jungle-print wallpaper as the backdrop for a vast collection of sunburst mirrors and clocks (each framed in a halo of gold plaster, brass, or spikes of teak). Flamenco dolls dance around vases of plastic foliage; trails of garlands, à la *South Pacific,* hang in the windows; and a lurid-green-painted mantelpiece, of late-19th-century origin, is loaded with personal mementoes – gilded angels, Elvis candles, roses, hearts, flowers, and other gift-shop souvenirs.

Andrew (a former lingerie merchandiser for a chain of department stores) and Craig (once a display designer) are the kind of fun guys who wear Hawaiian shirts as part of their daywear. They are known to friends for their "poptastic" parties (where even the garden statuary wears orange taffeta). They are also founders of Kitschen Sync (two London shops and a mail-order business), which used to sell "a glorious kitsch-a-rama of flashy trashy trinkets", until they decided to abandon the high street for a new career in wholesale.

They have since moved on to other things, but at one time Kitschen Sync supplied dozens of shops all over Britain with novelty party lights, squeezy tomato-ketchup bottles, plastic chandeliers, and Tretchikoff "green lady" table mats. And just to show they wouldn't dream of selling anything they couldn't live with themselves, every inch of their Victorian terraced house is furnished with a "tongue-in-chic" collection of vintage-meets-contemporary kitsch.

The Masson–McMinn kitchen is a homage to Miami, in ice-cream-coloured laminates, and furnished with flamingo shower curtains, strings of fake tropical fruit, and a 1950s-style dinette table, with matching chairs in sunny yellow vinyl trimmed with chrome. The bespoke diner-style kitchen was made for them by Al King, a London-based cabinet-maker who specializes in 1950s-style furniture. The floor is chequered with green and sky-blue ceramic tiles. The walls are turquoise and yellow; the paintwork is a hot, hot pink.

Their fearless use of colour knows no inhibitions – and even extends to the cloakroom under the stairs. This bright, brash cubicle is decorated with a Pop Art toilet seat and dozens of

The Miami-style "kitschen" is all summery Florida colours, 1950s-style diner furniture, flamingo curtains, and plastic fruit.

photographic snaps in vibrant plastic frames. The door is papered with a form of waterproof stick-on vinyl designed to cheer up boring black wheelie bins.

In the "Seventies Disco" bathroom, a sparkle-painted, roll-top tub sits on a raised platform surrounded by neat arrangements of glitter mirror balls, floor-to-ceiling mosaics, and psychedelic colours – yellow, green, turquoise, hot pink, scorching pink, and fuchsia. The ceiling is all distorted images reflected in mirror mosaics. The matching mirror above the bath-tub was bought in Ikea, but the swirly wallpaper above the tub is original 1970s vinyl. Another junk-shop find was the swivelling bucket chair, re-upholstered by Craig in two tones of red stretch-PVC.

The bathroom, he says, is the perfect place to relax with a lovely-jubbly glass of bubbly, listening to retro *Top of the Pops* albums, or the tropical fish-shaped radio. A bottle of "kitschy religious" Virgin Mary foam bath completes the picture.

A fearless use of colour extends to the shocking-pink cupboards in the kitchen, which were custom-made in plastic laminate and Cadillac-style chrome.

☞ The metallic feet of a sparkle-painted roll-top bath stand in a cluster of miniature dance-hall glitter balls on a sky-blue mosaic floor.

☞ With its mirrored mosaics and electric colours, the Seventies Disco bathroom is a place to chill out in a cool purple hot tub.

☞ The below-stairs toilet is a riot of florals and framed prints, furnished with a collage of holiday snaps, Pop Art seating, and a patriotic toilet roll.

Blissed Out

Tom Bliss is the kind of guy who leaves Christmas decorations up all year round. Not that anyone notices. The baubles and tinsel are barely distinguishable against the kaleidoscopic circus of colour that permeates every inch of his Hollywood apartment. Describing himself as an "art film guy" (artist, writer, film-maker, general poseur), Bliss comes from the "less is a bore" school of home decorating. Without colour, he says, he would wilt like an unwatered flower. His aesthetic owes something to the 1960s Pop Art movement, but it is pure self-expression: the product, he says, of a low budget, a little spare time, and "a heedless need for kitsch established early in life".

His playful Cloud Kitchen was knocked together using jigsawed plywood and Perspex (Lucite), mosaic tiles, and vitreous glass (plus three weekends of tedious cutting, gluing, and grouting). A seamstress friend (who, incidentally, makes masks for Mexican wrestlers in Tijuana), sewed clouds on sky-blue vinyl for the matching seats on the re-upholstered chrome stools. For his psychedelic

☞ A zigzag of poly-chrome emulsion frames *Satyr and Nymphs*, featuring Bliss and friends in woodland poses and pink wigs, painted in sequins, glitter, and saturated acrylics by "celebrated low-brow artist" Stacy Lande.

The heavenly Cloud Kitchen was an exercise in creative home decorating, put together from jigsawed plywood, mosaic tiles, and vinyl.

Overleaf left
Blissed-out hound
Boomerang (an alsation–
chow cross), is doggedly
tolerant of his master's
self-expressive aesthetic –
a jangling palette of
colour, pattern, and
Pop Art furniture.

Overleaf right
Hallucinogenic-style
hand-painted decor, with
vintage atomic lamp, and
a yellow fibreglass Egg
chair (complete with
built-in speakers), which
was a gift from one of
the It Twins (a blue-haired
club-kid music duo).

living room, Bliss spent months hand-cutting and sewing carpet (using skills learned during a brief stint as a carpet-layer in an earlier life) to create a complex mélange of colour and pattern, which continues up the painted walls to the ceiling and even over the windows. Co-ordinated furnishings include a 1970s futuristic Egg chair, a sputnik lamp, and an orange-plastic hand chair (a "knock-off" of a retro original). Bliss believes he suffers from "Gay Interior Decorator Syndrome", symptomatic of repressing innermost feelings while growing up in conventional society. "When you finally come out, it becomes all the more necessary to find a little space on earth that finally reflects you." Surprisingly, he's also into feng shui; or rather "the feng shui of kitsch – pure immediate gratification".

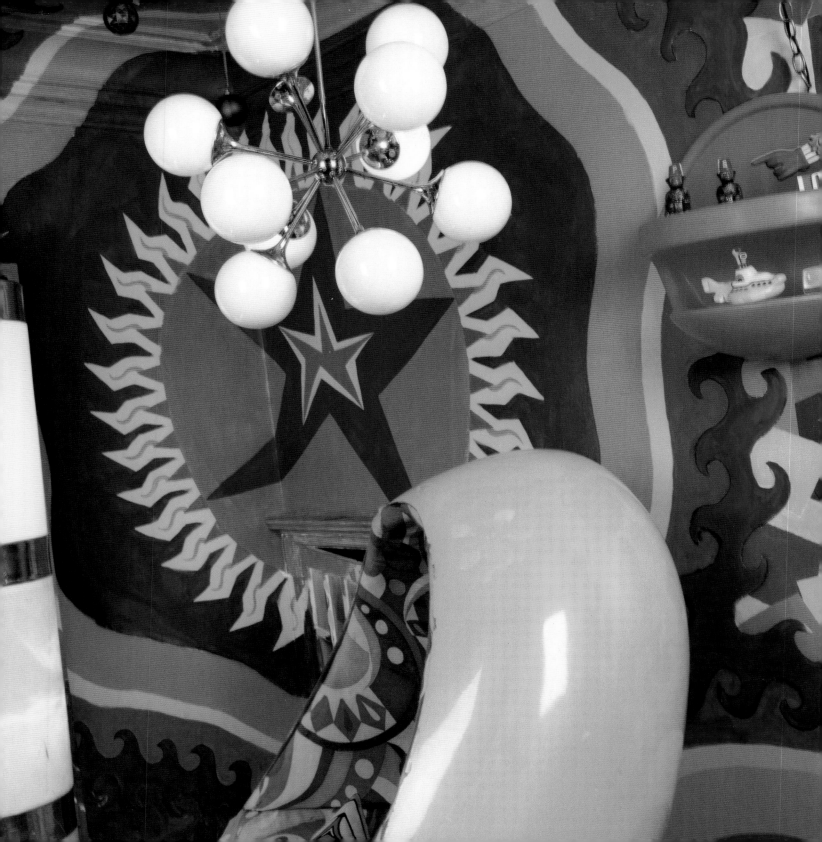

Holiday Home

The retro interior of Carolyn Shrosbree and James Lowe's 1968 house is testament to their joint obsession with collecting vintage kitsch. It reveals an element of professional interest, too (the couple run Flying Duck Enterprises, a shop dealing in 20th-century originals), but the impulse that drives most of their home-furnishing habits is a need to escape the dull, suburban world outside for another time, another place.

The squadrons of flying ducks that zoom across one yellow wall might indicate a yearning for the English countryside, but the couple's particular brand of escapism takes them much further afield. Indeed, with a few props and a bit of imagination, they can hop from a palm-fringed Hawaiian beach to a Californian-style cocktail bar, and from Las Vegas to outer space – without moving from the comfort of a zebra-print safari sofa, circa 1975.

Aside from James' huge collection of flying ducks (some 300 sets of three), the dominant feature of their living space is an enormous poster pasted onto one wall. Entitled *Sunny Palm Beach*, it enables them to lounge under a blue tropical sky, feet planted on beachy-yellow shag pile, while watching vintage movies on a space-age Grundig television set. Their three four-legged housemates – a Jack Russell called Presley, a black-and-white puss called Hilda (named after the

Cats Hilda and Sinclair sit around a limited-edition, 1970s Grundig television, while flocks of flying ducks head towards the coloured Formica landscape of a diner-style kitchen.

The dog's life for Presley is lounging on a zebra-print sofa beneath picture-poster palm trees and a blue Hawaiian sky.

character Hilda Ogden in the UK television programme *Coronation Street*), and a tiger-striped tom-cat called Sinclair (after inventor Clive Sinclair) – are never far away.

When it comes to buying, James and Carolyn's first priority is to stock their kitsch-collectables shop in Greenwich, London, but they are so into collecting themselves, they often find it hard to let things go. "If I find something I've never seen before, I usually end up keeping it," says Carolyn. "We also keep things that mean something to us, like the plastic pouffe I brought

☞ 1970s motel meets *Barbarella*, in a silver-lined glam-rock bedroom, furnished with fur fabric, shag pile, and a home-made platform bed.

☜ Behind the Californian cocktail bar is a wall of Tiki mugs, bamboo, fake stone-work, and an animated waterfall wall-light.

back from America, or the Elvis phone I found in Singapore." One of the things that James brought back from America is a keen interest in 1950s Tiki-bar culture. His Tiki-buying shopping trips to Los Angeles and Las Vegas (an exercise, he says, in "urban archaeology") have netted dozens of vintage mugs and mock-primitive carvings with a Pacific-island flavour. They are presented on bamboo shelves, framed in plastic stone-work (bought as part of a job-lot of 1970s wall-cladding, all unused and still in its original packaging), and set off by a wall-mounted electronic waterfall.

Along with a 1960s atomic lamp, and a modern mirror ball, the aforementioned Elvis phone has ended up in the couple's silver bedroom – where they have created a "space agey, *Barbarella*, 1970s-motel" look, with the liberal use of shag pile, white fake fur, and yards of metallic sequinned fabric, draped over all the vertical surfaces, and staple-gunned into place. "One of the reasons we use vintage furniture to create our own look is because we don't want our house to look like everyone else's," says Carolyn. "Nobody's going to walk in here and say, 'oh, this is just like my friend's place'."

Inside the Monsoon Wedding Karma Kar everything, from the rear-view mirror to the steering wheel and the seating, is upholstered with Indian textiles, and trimmed with braid.

Zen & the Art

The fastest way to reach India from London is to climb aboard a Karma Kar. The driver, or "karmonaut", will not need to travel far (indeed, he barely need switch on the engine), because his passengers will find themselves breathing in the atmosphere of the Indian sub-continent merely by opening the car door. A rich tapestry of saffron and terracotta silks, sequins, beads, and embroidery, scented with Nag Champa incense, and infused with the sitar twangings of raga music, the car is a little India on wheels.

A small fleet of "karma-ized" taxis, Karma Kars was founded by Tobias Moss, who dreamed up the idea while walking in the foothills of the Himalayas during one of his many trips to India. At the time, the Ambassador car, a lumbering chrome-bumpered saloon based on the classic Morris Oxford, and still made by Hindustan motors in Calcutta, was the predominant vehicle in India. "For me, it represented Indian motoring," says Tobias. However, he was able to buy his first three used Ambassadors in Britain. Later, the bureaucratic process of importing a new car from Calcutta to London took over a year to complete.

The name "Karma Kabs" came to Tobias in a dream, and seemed to him the perfect title for an enterprise that is guided by the Taoist philosophy that "the journey is more important than the destination". Kabs had to be changed to Kars when the public licensing office refused to accept the reference to cabs. Officially, therefore, Karma is not a taxi service, but a fleet of four chauffeur-driven cars available for private hire, "weddings, filming, and all lost causes".

The kars' customized interiors, which reflect the dashboard decorating habits of taxi drivers in Asia, evolved gradually: a flashing Ganesh (the divine Hindu protector) on the dashboard, a garland of plastic flowers on a bumper, a wisp of beaded chiffon in a rear window. When he met fellow Indiaphile Heather Allan, Tobias was so impressed by her ambitious ideas for his cars that he suggested she had a go at upgrading the decor. "She made such a great job of doing up my cars, I asked her to marry me," says Tobias.

Passengers are spiritually transported to Asia with the help of incense, music, and a tapestry of hand-made beading, Indian embroidery, and sequinned scarves.

This Ambassador car, based on an old Morris Oxford, and still made in Calcutta, has been "karma-ized" with garlands of plastic flowers.

Four Karma Kars (Bollywood, Monsoon Wedding, Tangerine Dream, and the Ab Fab Kab) feature Heather's handiwork, most of which entails sewing brightly coloured Indian textiles and baubles onto steering wheels and round petrol gauges. For the Monsoon Wedding ("a vision of regal splendour for gods and goddesses"), she lined the interior with embroidered tapestries bought in Indian bazaars. She added tinselled trimmings, miniature gods and dashboard deities, and glitter-studded scarves, all bought in Asian shops in London's Southall district. For the Bollywood she used images from classic film posters of the early 1970s, screen-printed onto fabric, mounted on velvet, and trimmed with gold braid. Hours of painstaking beading went into her home-made chandeliers.

So, who travels in the Karma Kars? "All the Fs," says Tobias. "Everyone in the world of food, fashion, and film, plus the funky, the funny, and the foxy." Karma "kustomers" include an impressive roll-call of the famous, too – soccer star Ronaldo, tennis champion John McEnroe, American pop group REM, supermodel Kate Moss, and fashion designer Jean Paul Gaultier. Tobias also provided cars for actress Emily Mortimer's wedding, and once took the entire fleet to Paris for Fashion Week. "All journeys are considered," he says, adding that a Karma trip is the fastest way to "obtain Nirvana without the hardships".

Vintage movie posters, featuring Indian heart-throb Raj Kapoor, form the basis of the Bollywood Karma Kar.

A crucifix, some plastic wildlife, and a wall of gilded glitter make a shrine out of a pair of camp Pierre et Gilles mermen.

Technicolour Dream Pad

The work of the French art-photographers known simply as Pierre et Gilles is inspired by the stereotypes of religion and mythology, peppered with surrealism and homoeroticism, drenched with gaudy Technicolor, and lit up like a theatre set (complete with pantomime costumes). Their symbiotic talents (Pierre trained as a photographer, Gilles as an illustrator) combine to create a distinctive oeuvre of soft-focus glamour portraiture. Celebrities and models are reincarnated as fairy princesses, Madonnas, matadors, mermaids, devils, or exotic deities, and set in an ethereal fantasy world, trimmed with fluffy cotton-wool clouds, bubbles, spangled stars, and trellises of pink flowers. Their home is furnished in much the same manner, and certainly uses the same vocabulary. Indeed, their house-cum-studio in suburban Paris is a temple of popular culture and kitsch iconography – a wall-to-wall devotion to the Bollywood-meets-Disney imagery that characterizes their work.

The house of Pierre et Gilles is a contradictory mix of traditional French furniture, *Chinoiserie*, and overwhelming collections of cheap souvenirs. The latter, arranged like temple shrines, include camp images (of sailors or mermen), pop idols, matinee idols, Buddhas, Catholic crucifixes, and a Hindu pantheon. And, in the spirit of their art, the whole ensemble is decorated with walls of gold glitter, miles of tiny mosaic tiles, metres of fairy lights, and trailing strings of plastic fruit and flowers.

 Portraits of the artists Pierre (left) and Gilles preside over a cornucopia of kitsch, including portraits of Elvis and Michael Jackson, girlie pin-ups, and a Hindu pantheon.

Overleaf:
A wrought-iron spiral staircase, trimmed with fake foliage, fairy lights, and Chinese lanterns.

House of Fun

Shari Maryon's style is the product of a wild-and-free approach to decorating, and conforms to no rules. Every inch of the four-storey Victorian townhouse that she shares with husband Bill, and their five children, is awash with colour and pattern, slapped on with a free spirit and a confident hand. The walls, the ceilings, the woodwork, the radiators, and even the furniture have all been treated to spots and splodges, leopardskin-prints, and "friesian" effects (as in black-and-white cowhide), swirls, and wobbly stripes of paint. The kitchen, for example, is decorated with stencilled teapots, set in islands of lime green in a sea of deep pink. Shari simply can't tolerate a plain surface ("I don't do dull"), nor an empty corner, and her love of colour permeates everything in the house, from fabrics to garlands of fake flowers.

"When I was a little girl, I wanted a house like Tom and Jerry's," says Shari. "So when I grew up and had kids of my own I tried to make our house as fun as possible." Hence, the Maryons' home is one big playroom, crowded with toys, dolls, and animal shapes, and a fiesta of picture-book images in vivid toyland shades. In some rooms, you can barely cross the room without tripping over a Cabbage Patch doll, or a tableau of miniature Sylvanian families, but not all the toys belong to the children. Even in the grown-ups' bedroom, there is a make-believe quality to the decor.

This kiddy fun-house offers lots of thrifty ideas for low-budget nursery decorators – and it's much more practical than it looks. "Children are very hard on the decor, but infant hand-prints and stains can easily be disguised with splodges of paint," explains Shari.

☞ In Shari and Bill's bedroom, a hand-painted leopardskin-print ceiling, matching woodwork, and orange-and-lemon striped walls set off a traditional brass bed, covered in pretty patchwork.

☞ The kitchen walls are decorated with stencilled teapots, each set in a splodge of green and a wash of wild fuchsia paint. Furnishings include hand-made pictorial shelves, flowery fabrics, painted chairs, and lots of colourful knick-knacks.

Saturday Night Fever

For Jim Pooke and Alan Radford, collecting kitsch is a compulsive habit that eats up much of their cash, and most of their spare time. Unable to resist a plastic-pineapple ice bucket, or a special-edition lava lamp, they spend their weekends shopping for the classics of chainstore kitsch. Never mind if they already have one (a set of Babycham glasses, perhaps, or a Tretchikoff print), there is always room for another. Thus, they have created the ultimate playboy pad, furnished in an over-the-top style, which strives to look as "outrageously kitsch as possible". Caught somewhere between 1950 and 1977, it is all the more surprising for being so utterly at odds with the London brick Victorian house that comes with Jim's school-caretaking job.

Behind a conventional front door, the house is an explosion of pinks and oranges, jungle-print, and glitter. First stop is the "good-time room" – a happy-hour space, furnished with nightclub neon, nylon tiger fur, and a pair of vintage cocktail bars in glitzy gold vinyl. Bar accessories include mirror balls, bead curtains, and hundreds of glasses (65 sets of six at the last count), plus a collection of novelty-shaped miniatures, musical decanters, and plastic-coated vino bottles, reminiscent of Mediterranean holidays circa 1965. Jim believes that his "addiction to kitsch" is all about rekindling memories, but as one of six children in a working-class East End

☞ Part of a 1970s Italian bedroom suite in playboy orange suede and smoked glass, an illuminated dressing table teams up with black shag pile, nodding dogs, and "nice-but-naff" art by Stephen Pearson.

☜ Beyond the patchwork-leather seating, the pink-painted kitchen is draped in Lurex, plastic fruit, and fairy lights.

family, it is more often about remembering things that other people had. "I was particularly jealous of a friend's Rolf Harris stylophone," he recalls. When he met Alan (who was brought up, he says, with "original kitsch"), their respective memories inspired a nostalgic "über-kitsch" style – an exaggerated version of the homes of their childhood: homes with glassy mirrored cabinets ("for displaying your posh bits, like your Spanish flamenco dancers"), and where the Tretch print was given pride of place.

Jim and Alan's lounge, furnished with an L-shaped arrangement of modular seating in patchwork leather, is sectioned from the pink kitchen with a freestanding room divider. Smoked-glass tables and shelves are loaded with a collection of over-sized brandy glasses, and at least 18 vintage lava lamps, including a 1960s Astro model, a giant Lunar, and a Glitter Baby. In the bedroom, Jim has used one wall as a canvas for a hand-painted monochrome mural. Based on *Geometri I*, by Danish designer Verner Panton, it goes rather well with the couple's Italian bedroom suite – a matching bed and dressing table upholstered in orange suede, with tinted-glass mirrors, and built-in lights. Jim and Alan have, of course, added their own touches – more glasses, more lava lamps, and, another kitsch classic, nodding dogs.

Boys' Toys

A strange brew of collectable mid-century modern furniture, Pop Art, trashy Big-Eye art, and a dash of American diner, all converging on the ground floor of a lofty, early-Victorian townhouse, Julian and Jakki Pransky-Poole's urban apartment is not an easy place to define. To add to the mix, they live with a family of disabled mannequins, a large tom-cat called Marilyn, a Spiderman, a couple of old-generation Star Trekkers, and the entire cast of *The Partridge Family*. An addiction to the 1970s is clearly displayed in an impressive collection of original toys and TV memorabilia (with a "space-agey vibe"), but they manage to strike a balance between kitsch collectables and the clean white space associated with contemporary modernism.

☞ Shelves of 1970s mugs and popular TV-show memorabilia, including *Bugs Bunny*, *The Flintstones*, and *The Partridge Family*.

☞ A Victorian fireplace is the centrepiece of a period living room furnished with 1960s–'70s classics (like the space-age television and the white Bonetto table), Pop Art, kitsch collectables, and cartoon lunch boxes.

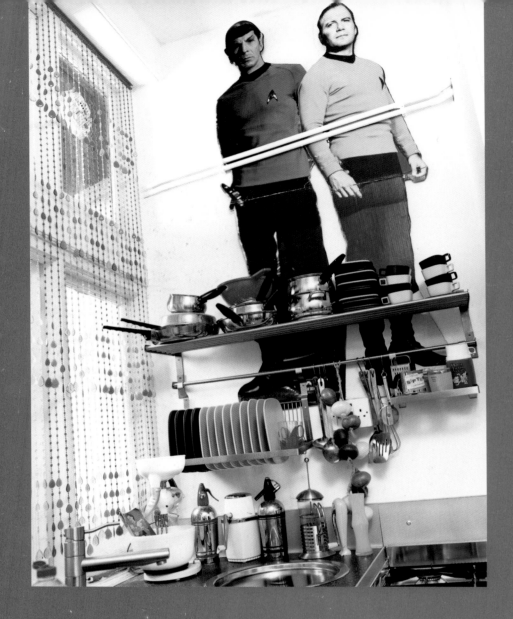

☞ Spiderman hovers above a modern retro-style red Smeg fridge, a collection of old Pepsi bottles, and a Harlem Globetrotters glass end-panel made for a pinball machine.

☜ Cardboard cut-outs of Star Trekkers Mr. Spock and Captain Kirk, wall-mounted above a diner-style stainless-steel kitchen.

The eclectic nature of the Pransky-Poole household can be explained partly by the couple's Anglo-American relationship. Julian, a British-born web designer and musician (he is the lead guitarist with Alison Moyet's band), met Jakki in her native California while working in Los Angeles. When they married, and moved to England, Jakki (who runs vintage clothiers Dolly Rockers, based in Selfridges, London) brought her huge collection of 1960s–'70s American furniture with her. "It all came over on a big boat," recalls Julian. Indeed, even the cat is Californian; although Julian's cardboard cut-outs of Captain Kirk, Mr. Spock, and Spiderman were bought in the UK, as was the red Smeg fridge, and a Fluidium lava lamp. So there are influences from both sides of the Atlantic.

The apartment's architecture is traditional English (stripped-wood floors, high ceilings, sash windows, an original fireplace), with contemporary touches – like a custom-made cast-iron grate, illuminated with coils of fairy lights. The furniture includes vintage chairs by Saarinen and Herman Miller, a 1969 plastic table by Rodolfo Bonetto, and a collector's edition Aphelion television – a reproduction of a space-age original designed by Stephen Foster in the early 1970s. A *Sunday B Morning* edition of Warhol's *Marilyn* is set incongruously among examples of kitschy art and poodle ornaments, a *Planet of the Apes* dustbin, a David Cassidy jigsaw puzzle, and a collection of themed lunch boxes (*How the West Was Won*, Marvel Comic "super powers", *Little House on the Prairie*, *Star Wars*, and *Indiana Jones*).

In the space-age diner-style kitchen, a Victorian cabinet is stuffed with more 1970s pop and TV memorabilia, including McDonald's freebie drinking glasses, cheap plastic cartoon figures (Fred Flintstone, Tweetie Pie, Bugs Bunny, Bart Simpson), and mementoes of cheesey television shows like *The Partridge Family, Charlie's Angels*, and *The Six Million Dollar Man*. Julian's love of "quality" British kitsch, meanwhile, is saved for the apartment's tiny hallway, where a little gallery of J.H. Lynch portraits hang on deep fuchsia walls over a 1950s hallstand, made of diaphanous plastic, quilted vinyl, and plastic flowers.

☞ A one-legged mannequin (in vintage shades) leans against an original *Star Trek* pinball machine, which is in full working order.

☜ Julian's magenta-painted hallway is a tiny gallery devoted to 1970s prints of exotic girlie paintings by J.H. Lynch, a 1950s wireware coat rack, and a vinyl-padded hallstand (plus plastic swans).

Punk Rococo

If kitsch means "to collect junk from the street" (as defined in some dictionaries), then artist and sculptor David Harrison is a true arbiter of the kitsch aesthetic. A self-confessed junk junkie, his home is largely furnished with found objects, scavenged from skips, dumps, and other repositories of discarded household detritus. "I can spend an hour poring over a skip," he admits, adding that he often sets off on a skip trip with a handcart to carry home his spoils. He prides himself on his ability to recognize hidden treasure (like one end of "a fab wrought-iron lamp" poking out of a pile of rubbish), but he is not overly fussy about its age or condition. "My home has become an orphanage for broken chairs", he says.

With a bit of ingenuity and a lot of gold spray-paint, David has turned decorating on a budget into a fine art. He calls it "Punk Rococo", but he doesn't really go in for definitions: "Decorating is not about a scheme, a colour, or a period, it's about finding things you like and

☞ A wall of cheap 1930s mirrors adds an extra dimension to a tiny bathroom, furnished with vintage fishy wallpaper, and a sea of plastic-dolly mermaids.

☜ David's galley kitchen is decorated with sticky-back plastic, splodges of paint, twiddles of wrought iron, and cute kitschy pictures.

☞ A dull pre-war dressing table is dressed up with a mix of rococo angels, recycled skip treasures, and more gold spray paint.

☜ David's much-loved poodle, Little Angel, sits on a bed of fake cat fur, beneath a collection of tasselled lamp-shades, spray-painted gilt mirrors, cherubs, and candelabra lights.

throwing them together," he says. The things he likes include "swirly bits and tassels", jungle-print fake fur, vintage wallpaper, mirrors, magenta and vermilion emulsion, dolls, cheap toys, and gold cherubs ("I always stock up on cherubs at Christmas – they are so much cheaper"). All of this is thrown together in the East London home he shares with his beloved black poodle, Little Angel. Incongruously, the raw material is a Victorian house sandwiched between a flyover and an industrial wasteland in the East End where David was born. "I always wanted to live on a flyover," he says – and this one has added cachet as the alleged grave of one the Kray twins' victims.

Typical of David's scrapyard decor is the "big drab" 1930s dressing table in his bedroom, which he customized by adding a scallop-shaped plastic pool liner found in a skip, an assortment of angels, flowers, bows, and broken dolls, and a liberal spraying of gold paint. "I don't see it as kitsch," he says. "Camp, yes, but not kitsch."

Directory

Shopping
UK

Flying Duck Enterprises
320–322 Creek Road
Greenwich
London SE10 9SW
Tel: +44 (0)20 8858 1964
1950s–'70s kitsch originals and decorative arts
(*see* pages 110–113)

A Garage Sale
Unit 1, 20 Wellington Lane
Montpelier
Bristol BS6 5PY
Tel: +44 (0)7951 269417 or (0)7989 515061
Original 1950s–'70s clothes, furniture, and accessories; open every Saturday, and by appointment

Her House
30D Great Sutton Street
London EC1V 0DU
Tel: +44 (0)20 7689 0606
1950s–'70s collectables

The JukeBox Shop
14 High Street
Lye
West Midlands DY9 8JT
Tel: +44 (0)1384 424325
www.thejukeboxshop.co.uk
1950s-style jukeboxes, diner furniture, neon signs, and memorabilia

Mary Rose Young
Oak House
Parkend
Lydney
Gloucestershire GL15 4JQ
Tel: +44 (0)1594 563425
Exuberant hand-made ceramics
(*see* pages 74–79)

Planet Bazaar
149 Drummond Street
London NW1 2PB
Tel: +44 (0)20 7387 8326
Retro collectables

Radio Days
87A Lower Marsh
Waterloo
London SE1 7AB
Tel: +44 (0)20 7928 0800
1940s–'70s memorabilia

Raw Deluxe
148 Gloucester Road
Bishopston
Bristol BS7 8NT
Tel: +44 (0)117 942 6998
Furniture and collectables, 1950s–'70s

Repsycho
85 Gloucester Road
Bristol BS7 8AS
Tel: +44 (0)117 983 0007
Retro fashions and home furnishings, from 1950s–'70s

Sparkle Moore
Alfie's Antiques Market
13–25 Church Street
London NW8 8DT
Tel: +44 (0)20 7724 8984
1950s fashions and household items

USA

Do Wah Diddy
3642E Thomas Road
Phoenix
AZ 85018
Tel: +1 602 957 3874
www.dowahdiddy.com
20th-century pop culture collectables

Go-Kat-Go
4832 West Glendale Avenue
Glendale
AZ 85301
Tel: +1 623 931 4926
www.go-kat-go.com
Specialists in Tiki, Hot-rod, and vintage kitsch

Kooky Kitsch
1715 Otis Drive
Alameda
CA 94501
www.kookykitsch.com
The offbeat, the obsolete, and the odd

JetsetModern
Broadway Antique Market
6130 North Broadway
Chicago
IL 60660
Tel: +1 773 743 5444
www.jetsetmodern.com

Vintage Castle

1048 Rosetree Lane

Cincinnati

OH 45230

Tel: +1 866 526 7577

www.vintagecastle.com

Swell 1950s items

Vintage Vending

288 North Broadway

Salem

NH 03079

Tel: +1 603 898 7676

www.vintagevending.com

Classic diner furniture and accessories, 1950s icons, and retro kitsch

Places to Visit
UK

Andrew Logan Museum of Sculpture

Berriew

Nr Welshpool

Powys SY21 8PJ

Tel: +44 (0)1686 640689

www.andrewlogan.com

Flamboyant sculpture from the artist and founder of the Alternative Miss World competition

South London Pacific

340 Kennington Road

London SE11 4LD

Tel: +44 (0)207 820 9189

www.southlondonpacific.com

Tiki theme-bar and night club

Zandra Rhodes Fashion and Textile Museum

83 Bermondsey Street

London SE1 3XF

Tel: +44 (0)20 7403 0222

www.ftmlondon.org

A showcase of vintage and modern fashions and textiles (*see* pages 86–91)

USA

Dollywood

1020 Dollywood Lane

Pigeon Forge

TN 37863

Tel: +1 865 428 9488

www.dollywood.com

Dolly Parton theme park (*see* page 51)

Graceland

3734 Elvis Presley Boulevard

Memphis

TN 38116

Tel: +1 901 527 6900

www.elvis.com

Liberace Museum

1775 East Tropicana Avenue

Las Vegas

NV 89119

Tel: +1 702 798 5595

www.liberace.com

Museum of Bad Art

10 Vogel Street

Boston

MA 02132

Tel: +1 617 325 8224

www.glyphs.com/moba

"Art too bad to be ignored"

Museum of Neon Art

501 West Olympic Boulevard

Los Angeles

CA 90015

Tel: +1 213 489 9918

www.neonmona.org

The Mystery Castle

Mystery Castle Foundation

PO Box 8265

800 East Mineral Road

Phoenix

AZ 85040

Tel: +1 602 268 1581

See pages 80–85

Places to Stay
UK

Hotel Pelirocco

10 Regency Square

Brighton BN1 2FG

Tel: +44 (0)1273 327055

www.hotelpelirocco.co.uk

18 bedrooms created by artists, maverick musicians, and cult fashion labels

USA

Caliente Tropics

411 East Palm Canyon Drive

Palm Springs

CA 92264

Tel: +1 760 327 1391

www.calientetropics.com

A Polynesian themed motel, founded 1964 (with regular Tiki weekends)

Madonna Inn

100 Madonna Road

San Luis Obispo

CA 93405

Tel: +1 805 543 3000

www.madonnainn.com

Queen of the themed hotels (*see* page 28)

Movie Colony

726 North Indian Canyon Drive

Palm Springs

CA 92262

Tel: +1 760 320 6340

www.moviecolony.com

Deco hotel with cool retro rooms dedicated
to surfing, Jackson Pollock, Marilyn Monroe,
Judy Garland, and 1950s style

Pelican Hotel

826 Ocean Drive

Miami Beach

FL 33139

Tel: +1 305 673 3373

www.pelicanhotel.com

"A myth in its own limelight" – Deco hotel
run by Diesel Jeans, with themed rooms
furnished with 1950s–'60s kitsch

The Shady Dell Trailer Park

1 Old Douglas Road

Bisbee

AZ 85603

Tel: +1 520 432 3567

www.theshadydell.com

Vintage aluminium trailers furnished with
1950s themed decor (*see* pages 54–61)

Useful Websites Miscellaneous

Bad Taste Unlimited

www.badtaste.nl

Kitschy images, camp clothes, tacky text,
bad-taste parties, and more

Classic Cafés

www.classiccafes.co.uk

A trip round London's greatest vintage
Formica cafés

Font Diner

www.fontdiner.com

On-line retro font shop (including
free downloads)

Karma Kars

www.karmakabs.com

Tel: +44 (0)20 8933 7052

Karma-ized Bollywood themed hire cars
(*see* pages 114–117)

Kitty Litter Design

www.kittylitterdesign.com

Wacky website design by Julian Pransky-Poole
(*see* pages 128–133)

Painting by Number

www.paintbynumberz.com

All you need to know about the Painting
by Number phenomenon (*see* page 49)

Tom Bliss

www.tombliss.com

Film-maker, model, artist (*see* pages 106–109)

World of Kitsch

www.worldofkitsch.com.

A tribute to all things tack

Shopping Online

Atomic Tiki

www.atomic-tiki.com

The coolest retro shop on the net
(mid-century, Tiki, Rockabilly, and vintage kitsch)

FiftieFiftie

www.fiftie-fiftie.be

20th-century modern design
and decorative arts

Flamingo Mania

www.flamingomania.com

All things flamingo-shaped

French Kitty

www.frenchkitty.co.uk

Cat's Meow clothing and accessories
(*see* page 31)

Genie's Fab Fabrics

www.thebrighton.demon.co.uk

Original textiles, 1950s–'70s

Hanford Lemoore's Tiki Room

www.tikiroom.com

Tiki fans hang-out – including
Tiki Central 24-hour store

Jesus Dress Up

www.jesusdressup.com

... and other dress-up fridge magnets

Mathmos, UK

www.mathmos.co.uk

Lava Lamps and other funky lighting

Modcity

www.gomod.com

The online magazine for modern objects, culture, and design

Off the Deep End

www.offthedeepend.com

... more flamingos

Poster Shop

www.postershop.com

Prints by Tretchikoff (*see* page 25) and Stephen Pearson (*see* page 6)

Presents Direct

www.presentsdirect.com

Tel: +44 (0)20 8246 4355

Online and mail-order gift shop

RetroFunk

www.retrofunk.com

Tel: +1 512 266 8935

Funky collectables from the Atomic age

Retro Kitsch Shop

www.kitsch.co.uk

Tel: +44 (0)1342 893947

Specialists in popular culture

Shag Art

www.shag-art.com

Collectible Tiki-moderne prints by Shag (*see* page 34)

Uptown Flamingo

www.uptownflamingo.com

... even more flamingos

Online Tourism

Bobs World of Liberace

www.bobsliberace.com

Tongue-in-cheek guide to the Liberace lifestyle (*see* page 43)

Butlins Memories

www.butlinsmemories.com

Celebrating the memories, history, and fun of Butlins (*see* page 29)

Neuschwanstein Castle, Bavaria

www.neuschwanstein.com/english

Online tours and visitors' handbook

Thunderbirds

www.thunderbirdsonline.com

Official fan site

Villa Velour

www.scn.org/villavelour

Museum of Velvet Painting (*see* page 43)

Bibliography

Banham, Mary and Hillier, Bevis
A Tonic to the Nation (Thames and Hudson, 1976)

Barratt, Helena and Phillips, John
Suburban Style (Macdonald & Co, 1987)

Carnot, Lélie
Collectible Snowdomes (Flammarion, 2002)

Cross, Robert
The Classic 1000 Cocktails (Foulsham, 2002)

Greenberg, Cara
Mid-century Modern: Furniture of the 1950s (Thames & Hudson, 1995)

Higgins, Katherine
Collecting the 1970s (Miller's, 2001)

Kirsten, Sven A.
The Book of Tiki (Taschen, 2000)

Maranian, Matt
Pad: The Guide to Ultra-Living (Chronicle, 2000)

Marsh, Madelaine
Collecting the 1950s (Miller's, 1997)

Marsh, Madelaine
Collecting the 1960s (Miller's, 1999)

Olalquiaga, Celeste
The Artificial Kingdom (Bloomsbury, 1999)

Parr, Martin (introduction)
Our True Intent Is All For Your Delight: The John Hinde Butlin's Photographs (Boot, 2002)

Sparke, Penny
A Century of Design (Mitchell Beazley, 1998)

Ward, Peter
Kitsch in Sync: A Consumer's Guide to Bad Taste (Plexus, 1994)

Index

Special thanks from the author to:

Josh Agle (aka "Shag"), Tom Bliss (and his dog, Boomerang), Kari French, Ed and Rita at the Shady Dell, Mary Lou Gulley, Brian Lewis, Brandi Kvetco and Chris Swanberg, David Harrison, Jim Pooke and Alan Radford, Julian and Jakki Pransky-Poole, Pierre et Gilles, Shari Maryon and family, Craig Masson and Andrew McMinn, Tobias Moss and Heather Allan, Carolyn Shrosbree, James Lowe and their model dog, Presley, Dale Sizer, Lucie Smailes (for her Kitsch Deluxe home, her excellent styling abilities, and the loan of a kitty-kitsch waste bin), Mary-Rose Young and Phil Butcher (and Malcolm, the cat), Zandra Rhodes, and everyone at the Fashion and Textile Musem in London, Alex and Phyllis Madonna at the Madonna Inn, CA, The Pelican Hotel at Miami Beach FL, Peter Hitchen (for the use of his garden gnome), Sven "Tiki" Kirsten, and Emily Anderson, Auberon Hedgecoe, and Giulia Hetherington at Mitchell Beazley (for their tolerance and endless patience).

Photographic Acknowledgments

All photographs are by Dave Young, with the exception of the following:

6 By courtesy of Felix Rosenstiel's Widow & Son Ltd, London/artist: Stephen Pearson; **6–7** Rex Features/Sipa; **8** Album/El Deseo S.A./Garrido, Amparo; **10** AKG London; **11** Bridgeman Art Library/Lauros/Giraudon/Private Collection © Andy Warhol Foundation for the Visual Arts, Inc/ARS, New York and DACS, London 2003; **12, 13** Philippe Garner; **14** Advertising Archives; **15** Memphis; **16–17** Alamy/Cindy Lewis; **20** Corbis/Alan Schein Photography; **21** Alamy/Mark Lewis; **26** Philippe Garner; **27** London Features International/Carlton International Media Ltd; **28** Corbis/Macduff Everton; **29** John Hinde Ltd/Chris Boot, photo Edmund Nagele; **32** Elvis image used by permission, Elvis Presley Enterprises, Inc; **34** Josh Agle (www.shag.com); **35** Sven A. Kirsten; **42** Kobal Collection; **43** Corbis/Bettman; **44 below** John Hinde Ltd; **47** Octopus Publishing Group Ltd/Ian Booth/Christie's; **50** © 2003 Mattel, Inc. All Rights Reserved; **51** Getty Images; **118–121** Deidi Von Schaewen; **134–137** Ray Main/Mainstream/artist David Harrison.

The publishers would also like to thank the following people for their help with photography for the opening sections of the book:

Front Jacket Lucie Smailes; **18** Shari Maryon; **22** Lucie Smailes; **24** Jim Pooke and Alan Radford; **30, 31** Lucie Smailes; **33, 36** Flying Duck Enterprises; **37** Lucie Smailes; **38** Mary-Rose Young and Phil Butcher; **40, 41, 46** Craig Masson and Andrew McMinn; **48** Brian Lewis; **49** Julian and Jakki Pransky-Poole; **52** Flying Duck Enterprises; **52–53** Kari French.